A LIFE OF
PRAYER

A LIFE OF PRAYER

A COLLECTION

OF WRITINGS FROM

GREAT CHRISTIAN AUTHORS

WHITAKER
HOUSE

A LIFE OF PRAYER
(Timeless Christian Classics series)

ISBN: 978-1-64123-382-8
eBook ISBN: 978-1-64123-383-5
Printed in the United States of America
© 2020 by Whitaker House

Whitaker House
1030 Hunt Valley Circle
New Kensington, PA 15068
www.whitakerhouse.com

Library of Congress Control Number: 2019953586

1 2 3 4 5 6 7 8 9 10 11 LU 27 26 25 24 23 22 21 20

CONTENTS

1

THE IMPORTANCE OF PRAYER

R.A. Torrey

In Ephesians 6:18, the tremendous importance of prayer is expressed with startling and overwhelming force: *"Praying always with all prayer and supplication in the Spirit, and watching thereto with all perseverance and supplication for all saints."* When the perceptive child of God stops to weigh the meaning of these words, then notes the connection in which they are found, he or she is driven to say, "I must pray, pray, pray. I must put all my energy and heart into prayer. Whatever else I do, I must pray."

Notice the alls: *"all prayer and supplication...all perseverance...for all saints."* Note the piling up of strong words: *"prayer," "supplication," "perseverance."* Also notice the strong expression, *"watching thereto,"* more literally, "in this, be not lazy." Paul realized the natural apathy of man, especially his natural neglect in prayer. How seldom we pray things through! How often the church and the individual get right up to the verge of a great blessing in prayer and then let go, become lazy, and quit. I wish that these words "in this, be not lazy" might burn into our hearts. I wish that the whole verse would burn into our hearts.

THE NECESSITY OF PERSISTENT PRAYER

Why is this constant, persistent, sleepless, overcoming prayer so necessary? Because there is a devil. He is cunning; he is mighty; he never rests; he is continually plotting the downfall of the children of God. If the children of God relax in prayer, the devil will succeed in ensnaring them.

Ephesians 6:12–13 reads:

For we wrestle not against flesh and blood, but against principalities, against powers, against the rulers of the darkness of this world, against spiritual wickedness in high places. Wherefore take to you the whole armor of God, that you may be able to withstand in the evil day, and having done all, to stand.

Next follows a description of the different parts of the Christian's armor that we are to put on if we are to stand against Satan and his mighty schemes. Paul brings his message to a climax in Ephesians 6:18, telling us that to all else we must add prayer—constant, persistent, untiring, sleepless prayer in the Holy Spirit—or all will be in vain.

Prayer is God's appointed way for obtaining things. The reason we lack anything in life is due to a neglect of prayer. James pointed this out very forcibly: *"You have not, because you ask not"* (James 4:2). The secret behind the poverty and powerlessness of the average Christian is neglect of prayer.

Many Christians are asking, "Why is it that I progress so little in my Christian life?"

"Neglect of prayer," God answers. "You do not have because you do not ask."

Many ministers are asking, "Why is it I see so little fruit from my labors?"

Again, God answers, "Neglect of prayer. You do not have because you do not ask."

Many Sunday school teachers are asking, "Why is it that I see so few converted in my Sunday school class?"

Still, God answers, "Neglect of prayer. You do not have because you do not ask."

Both ministers and churches are asking, "Why is it that the church of Christ makes so little headway against unbelief, error, sin, and worldliness?"

Once more, we hear God answering, "Neglect of prayer. You do not have because you do not ask."

Those men whom God set forth as a pattern of what He expected Christians to be—the apostles—regarded prayer as the most important business of their lives. When the multiplying responsibilities of the early church crowded in upon them, this was the response of the twelve disciples:

> [They] *called the multitude of the disciples to them, and said, It is not reason that we should leave the word of God, and serve tables. Wherefore, brethren, look you out among you seven men of honest report, full of the Holy Ghost and wisdom, whom we may appoint over this business. But we will give ourselves continually to prayer, and to the ministry of the word.* (Acts 6:2–4)

From what Paul wrote to both churches and individuals, it is evident that much of his time, strength, and thought were devoted to prayer for them. (See Romans 1:9; Ephesians 1:15–16; Colossians 1:9; 1 Thessalonians 3:10; and 2 Timothy 1:3.) All the mighty men of God outside of those in the Bible have been men of prayer. They have differed from one another in many things, but in this practice of faithful praying, they have been alike.

THE MINISTRY OF INTERCESSION

Prayer occupied a very prominent place and played a very important part in the earthly life of our Lord. Turn, for example, to Mark 1:35: "In *the morning, rising up a great while before day, He went out, and departed into a solitary place, and there prayed."* The preceding day had been a very busy and exciting one, but Jesus shortened the hours of needed sleep so that He could rise early and give Himself to more sorely needed prayer.

Turn to Luke 6:12, where we read, *"And it came to pass in those days, that He went out into a mountain to pray, and continued all night in prayer to God."* Our Savior occasionally found it necessary to spend a whole night in prayer.

The words *pray* and *prayer* are used at least twentyfive times in connection with our Lord in the brief record of His life in the four Gospels, and His praying is mentioned in places where these words are not used. Evidently prayer took much of Jesus's time and strength. A man or woman who does not spend much time in prayer cannot properly be called a follower of Jesus Christ.

Praying is the most important part of the present ministry of our risen Lord. This reason for constant, persistent, sleepless, overcoming prayer seems, if possible, even more forcible than the others.

PRAYING IS THE MOST IMPORTANT PART OF THE PRESENT MINISTRY OF OUR RISEN LORD. THIS REASON FOR CONSTANT, PERSISTENT, SLEEPLESS, OVERCOMING PRAYER SEEMS, IF POSSIBLE, EVEN MORE FORCIBLE THAN THE OTHERS.

Christ's ministry did not end with His death. His atoning work was finished then, but when He rose and ascended to the right hand of the Father, He entered into other work for us, work just as important in its place as His atoning work. It cannot be separated from His atonement because it rests on that as its basis and is necessary to our complete salvation.

We read what that great, present work is by which He carries our salvation on to completeness: *"Wherefore He is able also to save them to the uttermost that come to God by Him, seeing He ever lives to make intercession for them"* (Hebrews 7:25). This verse tells us that Jesus is able to save us to the uttermost, not merely from the uttermost, but to the uttermost—to entire completeness and absolute perfection. He is able to do this not only because He died, but also because He "always lives."

The verse also tells us why He now lives: *"to make intercession"*—to pray. Praying is the principal thing He is doing in these days. It is by His prayers that He is saving us.

The same thought is found in Paul's remarkable, triumphant challenge: *"Who is he that condemns? It is Christ that died, yea rather, that is risen again, who is even at the right hand of God, who also makes intercession for us"* (Romans 8:34).

If we are to have fellowship with Jesus Christ in His present work, we must spend much time in prayer. We must give ourselves to earnest, constant, persistent, sleepless, overcoming prayer.

I know of nothing that has so impressed me with a sense of the importance of praying at all seasons—being much and constantly in prayer—as the thought that this is the principal occupation of my risen Lord even now. I want to have fellowship with Him. For that reason, I have asked the Father, whatever else He may make me, to make me an intercessor. I pray that He will make me a man who knows how to pray and who spends much time in prayer.

This ministry of intercession is glorious and mighty, and we can all have a part in it. The man or woman who cannot attend a prayer meeting because of illness can have a part in it. The busy mother and the woman who works outside the home can have a part. They can mingle prayers for the saints, for their pastor, for the unsaved, and for missionaries with their day's work. The harddriven man of business can have a part in it, praying as he hurries from duty to duty. But we must, if we want to maintain this spirit of constant prayer, take time—and plenty of it—when we shut ourselves up in the secret place alone with God for nothing but prayer.

RECEIVING MERCY, GRACE, AND JOY

Prayer is the means that God has appointed for our receiving mercy and obtaining grace. Hebrews 4:16 is one of the simplest, sweetest verses in the Bible: *"Let us therefore come boldly to the throne of grace, that we may obtain mercy, and find grace to help in time of need."* These words make it very clear that God has appointed a way by which we can seek and obtain mercy and grace. That way is prayer—a bold, confident, outspoken approach to the throne of grace, the most holy place of God's presence. There, our sympathizing High Priest, Jesus Christ, has entered in our behalf. (See Hebrews 4:14–15.)

Mercy is what we need, and grace is what we must have; otherwise, all our lives and efforts will end in complete failure. Prayer is the way to obtain mercy and grace. Infinite grace is at our disposal, and we make it ours by prayer. It is ours for the asking. Oh, if we only realized the fullness of God's grace—its height, depth, length, and breadth—I am sure we would spend more time in prayer. The measure of our appropriation of grace is determined by the measure of our prayers.

Who does not feel that he needs more grace? Then ask for it. Be constant and persistent in your asking. Be diligent and untiring in your asking. God delights in our persistence in prayer, for it shows our faith in Him, and He is mightily pleased with faith. Because of our perseverance, He will rise and give us as much as we need. (See Luke 11:8.) What little streams of mercy and grace most of us know when we might know rivers overflowing their banks!

Prayer in the name of Jesus Christ is the way He Himself has appointed for His disciples to obtain fullness of joy. He states this simply and beautifully: *"Until now have you asked nothing in My name: ask, and you shall receive, that your joy may be full"* (John 16:24). Who does not wish for joy? Well, the way to have full joy is by praying in the name of

Jesus. We all know people who are full of joy. Indeed, it is just running over, shining from their eyes, bubbling out of their very lips, and running off their fingertips when they shake your hand. Coming in contact with them is like coming in contact with an electrical machine charged with gladness. People of that sort are always people who spend much time in prayer.

Why is it that prayer in the name of Christ brings such fullness of joy? In part, because we get what we ask. But that is not the only reason, nor is it the greatest. Prayer makes God real. When we ask something definite of God, and He gives it, how real God becomes! He is right there! It is blessed to have a God who is real and not merely an idea. I remember once when I suddenly and seriously fell ill all alone in my study. I dropped on my knees and cried to God for help. Instantly, all pain left me, and I was perfectly well. It seemed as if God stood right there, reached out His hand, and touched me. The joy of the healing was not as great as the joy of meeting God.

No joy on earth or in heaven is greater than communion with God. Prayer in the name of Jesus brings us into communion with God. The psalmist was surely not speaking only of future blessedness, but also of present blessedness, when he said, *"In Your presence is fullness of joy"* (Psalm 16:11). Oh, the unutterable joy of those moments when, in our prayers, we really enter into the presence of God!

Does someone say, "I have never known joy like that in prayer"? Do you take enough leisure for prayer to actually sense God's presence? Do you really give yourself up to prayer in the time that you do take?

FREEDOM FROM ANXIETY

In every care, anxiety, and need of life, prayer with thanksgiving is the means that God has appointed for our obtaining freedom from all anxiety and the peace of God that passes all understanding. Paul said:

Be careful for nothing; but in every thing by prayer and supplication with thanksgiving let your requests be made known to God. And the

*peace of God, which passes all understanding, shall keep your hearts
and minds through Christ Jesus.*   (Philippians 4:6–7)

To many, this initially seems like the picture of a life that is beautiful but beyond the reach of ordinary mortals. This is not so at all. The verse tells us how this life of peace is attainable by every child of God: *"Be careful for nothing"* (verse 6). The remainder of the verse tells us how to do this. It is very simple: *"…but in every thing by prayer and supplication with thanksgiving let your requests be made known to God."*

What could be plainer or more simple than that? Just keep in constant touch with God. When troubles or afflictions—great or small—occur, speak to Him about it, never forgetting to return thanks for what He has already done. What will the result be? *"And the peace of God, which passes all understanding, shall keep your hearts and minds through Christ Jesus"* (verse 7).

That is glorious, and it is as simple as it is glorious! Thank God, many are trying it. Do you know anyone who is always serene? Perhaps this person has a very temperamental nature. Nevertheless, when troubles, conflicts, opposition, and sorrow sweep around him, the peace of God that is beyond all understanding will keep his heart and his thoughts in Christ Jesus.

We all know people like that. How do they do it? By prayer, that is how. They know the deep peace of God, the unfathomable peace that surpasses all understanding, because they are men and women of much prayer.

Some of us let the hurry of our lives crowd prayer out; what a waste of time, energy, and emotion there is in this constant worry! One night of prayer will save us from many nights of insomnia. Time spent in prayer is not wasted; it is time invested at a big interest.

VEHICLE FOR THE HOLY SPIRIT

Prayer is the method that God Himself has appointed for our obtaining the Holy Spirit. The Bible is very plain on this point. Jesus said,

"If you then, being evil, know how to give good gifts to your children how much more shall your Father which is in heaven give good things to them that ask Him?" (Matthew 7:11).

I know this as definitely as I know that my thirst is quenched when I drink water. Early one morning in the Chicago Avenue Church prayer room, where several hundred people had been assembled a number of hours in prayer, the Holy Spirit fell so fully that no one could speak or pray. The whole place was so filled with His presence that sobs of joy filled the place. Men left that room and went to different parts of the country, taking trains that very morning, and the effects of the outpouring of God's Holy Spirit in answer to prayer were soon reported. Others went into the city with the blessing of God on them. This is only one instance among many that might be cited from personal experience.

If we would only spend more time in prayer, there would be more fullness of the Spirit's power in our work. Many who once worked unmistakably in the power of the Holy Spirit now fill a room with empty shouting, beating the air with meaningless gestures, because they have neglected prayer. We must spend much time on our knees before God if we are to continue in the power of the Holy Spirit.

BE READY FOR HIS RETURN

Prayer is the means that Christ has appointed so that our hearts will not be overcome with indulgences, drunkenness, and the cares of this life, so that the day of Christ's return will not come upon us suddenly as a snare. (See Luke 21:34–35.) We are warned in Scripture: *"Watch you therefore, and pray always, that [we] may be accounted worthy to escape all these things that shall come to pass, and to stand before the Son of man"* (verse 36). According to this passage, there is only one way that we can be prepared for the coming of the Lord when He appears: through much prayer.

The second coming of Jesus Christ is a subject that is awakening much interest and discussion in our day. It is one thing to be interested in the Lord's return and to talk about it, but it is another thing to be prepared for it. We live in an atmosphere that has a constant tendency to make us unsuitable for Christ's coming. The world tends to draw us down by its self-indulgences and cares. There is only one way by which we can triumphantly rise above these things—by constant watching in prayer, that is, by sleeplessness in prayer. *"Watch"* in this passage is the same strong word used in Ephesians 6:18, and *"always"* means to pray at all times. The man who spends little time in prayer, who is not steadfast and constant in prayer, will not be ready for the Lord when He comes. But we can be ready. How? Pray! Pray! Pray!

THE WORLD TENDS TO DRAW US DOWN
BY ITS SELF-INDULGENCES AND CARES.
THERE IS ONLY ONE WAY BY WHICH WE CAN
TRIUMPHANTLY RISE ABOVE THESE THINGS—
BY CONSTANT WATCHING IN PRAYER, THAT IS,
BY SLEEPLESSNESS IN PRAYER.

WE NEED TO PRAY

Prayer is necessary because of what it accomplishes. Much has been said about that already, but more should be added. Prayer promotes our spiritual growth as almost nothing else, indeed, as nothing else except Bible study. Prayer and Bible study go hand in hand.

Through prayer, my sin—my most hidden sin—is brought to light. As I kneel before God and pray, *"Search me, O God, and know my heart: try me, and know my thoughts: and see if there be any wicked way in me"* (Psalm 139:23–24), God directs the penetrating rays of His light into the innermost recesses of my heart. The sins I never suspected to be present are brought to light. In answer to prayer, God washes away my iniquity and cleanses my sin. (See Psalm 51:2.) My eyes are opened to behold wondrous things out of God's Word. (See Psalm 119:18.) I receive wisdom to know God's way (see James 1:5) and strength to walk in it. As I meet God in prayer and gaze into His face, I am changed into His image "*from glory to glory*" (2 Corinthians 3:18). Each day of true prayer life finds me more like my glorious Lord.

John Welch, the soninlaw of John Knox, was one of the most faithful men of prayer this world has ever seen. He counted any day in which seven or eight hours were not devoted solely to God in prayer and the study of His Word as wasted time. An old man speaking of him after his death said, "He was a type of Christ." How did he become so like his Master? His prayer life explains the mystery.

Prayer also brings power into our work. If we wish power for any work to which God calls us, whether it is preaching, teaching, personal work, or the raising of our children, we can receive it by earnest prayer.

A woman, with a little boy who was perfectly incorrigible, once came to me in desperation and said, "What should I do with him?"

I asked, "Have you ever tried prayer?"

She said she had prayed for him, she thought. I asked if she had made his conversion and his character a matter of specific, expectant prayer. She replied that she had not been definite in the matter. She began that day, and at once there was a marked change in the child. As a result, he grew up into Christian manhood.

How many Sunday school teachers have taught for months and years and seen no real fruit from their labors? Then, they learn the secret of intercession; by earnest pleading with God, they see their students, one by one, brought to Christ! How many poor teachers have become mighty people of God by casting away their confidence in their own abilities and gifts and giving themselves up to God to wait on Him for the "*power from on high*" (Luke 24:49)! Along with other believers, the Scottish evangelist John Livingstone spent a night in prayer to God. When he preached the next day, five hundred people were either converted or marked some definite uplift in their spiritual lives. Prayer and power are inseparable.

Prayer avails for the conversion of others. Few people are converted in this world in any other way than in connection with someone's prayers. I previously thought that no human being had anything to do with my own conversion, for I was not converted in church or Sunday school or in personal conversation with anyone. I was awakened in the middle of the night and converted. As far as I can remember, I did not have the slightest thought of being converted, or of anything of that nature, when I went to bed and fell asleep. But I was awakened in the middle of the night and converted probably within five minutes. A few minutes before, I was about as near eternal damnation as one gets. I had one foot over the brink and was trying to get the other one over. As I said, I thought no human being had anything to do with it, but I had forgotten my mother's prayers. Later, I learned that one of my college classmates had decided to pray for me until I was saved.

Prayer often avails where everything else fails. How utterly all of Monica's efforts and entreaties failed with her son! But her prayers prevailed with God, and the immoral youth became St. Augustine, the mighty man of God. By prayer, the bitterest enemies of the gospel have become its most valiant defenders, the most wicked the truest sons of God, and the most contemptible women the purest saints. Oh, the power of prayer to reach down, where hope itself seems vain, and lift men and women up into fellowship with and likeness to God! It is simply wonderful! How little we appreciate this marvelous weapon!

Prayer brings blessings to the church. The history of the church has always been full of grave difficulties to overcome. The devil hates the church and seeks in every way to block its progress by false doctrine, by division, and by inward corruption of life. But by prayer, a clear way can be made through everything. Prayer will root out heresy, smooth out misunderstanding, sweep away jealousies and animosities, obliterate immoralities, and bring in the full tide of God's reviving grace. History abundantly proves this. In the darkest hour, when the state of the church has seemed beyond hope, believing men and women have met together and cried to God, and the answer has come.

It was so in the days of Knox, and in the days of Wesley, Whitefield, Edwards, and Brainerd. It was so in the days of Finney and in the days of the great revival of 1857 in this country and of 1859 in Ireland. And it will be so again in your day and mine! Satan has organized his forces. Some people, claiming great apostolic methods, are merely covering the rankest dishonesty and hypocrisy with their loud and false assurance. Christians equally loyal to the great fundamental truths of the gospel are scowling at one another with a devilsent suspicion. The world, the flesh, and the devil are holding a merry carnival. It is a dark day, but now *"it is time for You, Lord, to work: for they have made void Your law"* (Psalm 119:126). He is getting ready to work, and now He is listening for the voice of prayer. Will He hear it? Will He hear it from you? Will He hear it from the church as a body? I believe He will.

2

THE THRONE OF GRACE

Charles Spurgeon

The throne of grace. (Hebrews 4:16)

These words are found embedded in that gracious verse, "*Let us therefore come boldly to the throne of grace, that we may obtain mercy, and find grace to help in time of need*" (Hebrews 4:16). They are a gem in a golden setting. True prayer is an approach of the soul by the Spirit of God to the throne of God. It is not the utterance of words; it is not alone the feeling of desires; but it is the advance of the desires to God, the spiritual approach of our nature towards the Lord our God. True prayer is neither a mere mental exercise nor a vocal performance. It is far deeper than that. It is spiritual commerce with the Creator of heaven and earth.

God is a Spirit, unseen by mortal eye and only to be perceived by the inner man. Our spirit within us, begotten by the Holy Spirit at our regeneration, discerns the Great Spirit, communes with Him, sets before Him its requests, and receives from Him answers of peace. It is a spiritual business from beginning to end. Its aim and objective end not with man, but they reach to God Himself.

In order to offer such prayer, the work of the Holy Spirit Himself is needed. If prayer were of the lips alone, we would only need breath in our nostrils to pray. If prayer were of the desires alone, many excellent desires are easily felt, even by natural men. But when it is the spiritual desire and the spiritual fellowship of the human spirit with the Great Spirit, then the Holy Spirit Himself must be present all through it. He helps infirmity and gives life and power. Without the Holy Spirit, true prayer will never be presented; the thing offered to God will wear the name and have the form, but the inner life of prayer will be far from it.

Moreover, it is clear from the connection of our text that the interposition of the Lord Jesus Christ is essential to acceptable prayer. As prayer will not be truly prayer without the Spirit of God, so it will not be prevailing prayer without the Son of God. He, the Great High Priest, must go within the veil for us; no, through His crucified person the veil must be entirely taken away. Until then, we are shut out from the living God. The man who, despite the teaching of Scripture, tries to pray without our Savior, insults the Deity. He who imagines that his own natural desires, coming up before God, unsprinkled with the precious blood, will be an acceptable sacrifice before God, makes a mistake; he has not brought an offering that God can accept, any more than if he had struck off a dog's head or offered an unclean sacrifice. Worked in us by the Spirit, presented for us by the Christ of God, prayer becomes power before the Most High, but not by any other way.

In trying to write about the text, I will outline it this way: First, here is a throne. Second, here is grace. Then we will put the two together, and we will see grace on a throne. And putting them together in another order, we will see sovereignty manifesting itself and resplendent in grace.

A THRONE

Our text speaks of a throne, *"the throne of grace."* God is to be viewed in prayer as our Father; that is the aspect that is dearest to us. However, we are not to regard Him as though He were such as we are. Our Savior has qualified the expression *"our Father"* with the words *"in heaven"* (Matthew 6:9) close at the heels of that gracious name. He wanted to remind us that our Father is still infinitely greater than we are. He has bidden us say, *"Hallowed be Your name. Your kingdom come"* (Matthew 6:9–10), for our Father is still to be regarded as King. In prayer we come not only to our Father's feet, but also to the throne of the Great Monarch of the universe. The mercy seat is a throne, and we must not forget this.

LOWLY REVERENCE

If prayer should always be regarded by us as an entrance into the courts of the Royalty of heaven, if we are to behave ourselves as courtiers should in the presence of an illustrious majesty, then we are not at a loss to know the right spirit in which to pray. If in prayer we come to a throne, it is clear that we should, in the first place, approach in a spirit of lowly reverence. It is expected that the subject in approaching the king should pay him homage and honor. The pride that will not acknowledge the king, the treason which rebels against the sovereign will, should, if it is wise, avoid any near approach to the throne. Let pride bite the curb at a distance, let treason lurk in corners, for only lowly reverence may come before the King Himself when He sits clothed in His robes of majesty.

In our case, the King before whom we come is the highest of all monarchs, the King of Kings, the Lord of Lords. Emperors are but the shadows of His imperial power. They call themselves kings by right divine, but what divine right do they have? Common sense laughs their pretensions to scorn. The Lord alone has divine right, and to Him only does the kingdom belong. He is *"the blessed and only Potentate"* (1 Timothy 6:15). They are but nominal kings, to be set up and put down at the will of men or the decree of providence; but He is Lord alone, the Prince of the kings of the earth.

He sits on no precarious throne,
Nor borrows leave to be.

My heart, be sure that you prostrate yourself in such a presence. Since He is so great, place your mouth in the dust before Him, for He is the most powerful of all kings. His throne has sway in all worlds. Heaven obeys Him cheerfully, hell trembles at His frown, and earth is constrained to yield Him homage willingly or unwillingly. His power can make or can destroy. To create or to crush, either is easy enough to Him. My soul, be sure that when you draw nigh to the omnipotent God, who is as a consuming fire, you put your shoes from off your feet and worship Him with lowliest humility.

Besides, He is the most holy of all kings. His throne is a great, white throne, unspotted and clear as crystal. *"The heavens are not clean in His sight"* (Job 15:15), and *"His angels He charged with folly"* (Job 4:18). And you, a sinful creature, with lowliness you should draw near to Him. Familiarity there may be, but let it not be unhallowed. Boldness there should be, but let it not be impertinent. Still, you are on earth and He in heaven. Still, you are a worm of the dust, a creature *"crushed before the moth"* (Job 4:19), and He is the Everlasting. *"Before the mountains were brought forth…You are God"* (Psalm 90:2). If all created things should pass away again, still He would be the same. My friends, I am afraid we do not bow as we should before the Eternal Majesty; but, henceforth, let us ask the Spirit of God to put us in a right attitude, so that every one of our prayers may be a reverential approach to the Infinite Majesty above.

DEVOUT JOYFULNESS

A throne is, in the second place, to be approached with devout joyfulness. If I find myself favored by divine grace to stand among those favored ones who frequent His courts, should I not feel glad? I might have been in His prison, but I am before His throne. I might have been driven from His presence forever, but I am permitted to come near to Him, even into His royal palace, into His secret chamber of gracious audience. Should I not then be thankful? Should not my thankfulness ascend into joy, and should I not feel that I am honored, that I am made the recipient of great favors, when I am permitted to pray?

Why is your countenance sad, oh, suppliant, when you stand before the throne of grace? If you were before the throne of justice to be condemned for your iniquities, you might well be sad. But now you are favored to come before the King in His silken robes of love; let your face shine with sacred delight. If your sorrows are heavy, tell them to Him, for He can comfort you. If your sins are multiplied, confess them, for He can forgive them. Oh, courtiers in the halls of such a Monarch, be exceedingly glad, and mingle praises with your prayers.

COMPLETE SUBMISSION

It is a throne, and therefore, in the third place, whenever it is approached, it should be with complete submission. We do not pray to God to instruct Him as to what He ought to do; neither for a moment must we presume to dictate the line of the divine procedure. We are permitted to say to God, "Thus and thus would we have it," but we must evermore add, "But, seeing that we are ignorant and may be mistaken— seeing that we are still in the flesh and, therefore, may be actuated by carnal motives—not as we will, but as You will."

WE DO NOT PRAY TO GOD TO INSTRUCT HIM AS TO WHAT HE OUGHT TO DO; NEITHER FOR A MOMENT MUST WE PRESUME TO DICTATE THE LINE OF THE DIVINE PROCEDURE.

Who would dictate to the throne? No loyal child of God will for a moment imagine that he is to occupy the place of the King, but he bows before Him who has a right to be Lord of all. Though he utters his desire earnestly, vehemently, persistently, and pleads and pleads again, yet it is evermore with this needful reservation: "Your will be done, my Lord; and if I ask anything that is not in accordance with Your will, my inmost will is that You would be good enough to deny Your servant. I will take it as a true answer if You refuse me if I ask that which does not seem good in Your sight." If we constantly remembered this, I think we would be less inclined to push certain suits before the throne, for we would feel, "I am here in seeking my own ease, my own comfort, my own advantage, and, perhaps, I may be asking for that which would dishonor God. Therefore, I will speak with the deepest submission to the divine decrees."

ENLARGED EXPECTATIONS

Friends, in the fourth place, if it is a throne, it ought to be approached with enlarged expectations. Well does our hymn put it:

> Thou art coming to a king:
> Large petitions with thee bring.

We do not come in prayer, as it were, only to God's poorhouse where He dispenses His favors to the poor, nor do we come to the back door of the house of mercy to receive the broken scraps, though that would be more than we deserve; to eat the crumbs that fall from the Master's table is more than we could claim. But, when we pray, we are standing in the palace on the glittering floor of the great King's own reception room, and thus we are placed upon a vantage ground. In prayer we stand where angels bow with veiled faces. There, even there, the cherubim and seraphim adore before that selfsame throne to which our prayers ascend. And should we come there with stunted requests and narrow and contracted faith? No, it does not become a King to be giving away pennies and nickels; He distributes pieces of gold. He scatters not, as poor men must, scraps of bread and broken meat, but He makes a feast of fat things, of fat things full of marrow, of wines well refined.

Take heed of imagining that God's thoughts are as your thoughts and His ways as your ways. (See Isaiah 55:8.) Do not bring small petitions and narrow desires before God and say, "Lord, do according to these." Remember, as high as the heavens are above the earth, so high are

His ways above your ways, and His thoughts above your thoughts. (See Isaiah 55:9.) Ask, therefore, after a godlike sort. Ask for great things, for you are before a great throne. Oh, that we always felt this when we come before the throne of grace, for then He would do for us *"exceeding abundantly above all that we ask or [even] think"* (Ephesians 3:20).

UNSTAGGERING CONFIDENCE

And, beloved, I may add, in the fifth place, that the right spirit in which to approach the throne of grace is that of unstaggering confidence. Who would doubt the King? Who dares impugn the Imperial word? It was well said that if integrity were banished from the hearts of all mankind besides, it ought still to dwell in the hearts of kings. Shame on a king if he can lie. The beggar in the streets is dishonored by a broken promise, but what can we say of a king if his word cannot be depended upon?

Oh, shame on us if we are unbelieving before the throne of the King of heaven and earth. With our God before us in all His glory, sitting on the throne of grace, will our hearts dare to say we mistrust Him? Will we imagine either that He cannot or will not keep His promise? There, surely, is the place for the child to trust his father, for the loyal subject to trust his monarch; therefore, all wavering or suspicion should be far from the throne. Unstaggering faith should be predominant before the mercy seat.

DEEPEST SINCERITY

I have only one more remark to make on this point: if prayer is a coming before the throne of God, it ought to always be conducted with the deepest sincerity and in the spirit that makes everything *real*. If you are disloyal enough to despise the King, at least, for your own sake, do not mock Him to His face and when He is upon His throne. If anywhere you dare repeat holy words without heart, let it not be in Jehovah's palace. If I am called upon to pray in public, I must not dare use words that are intended to please the ears of my fellow worshipers, but I must realize that I am speaking to God Himself and that I have business to transact with the great Lord. And, in my private prayer, if I rise from my bed in the morning and bow my knee and repeat certain words, or if go through the same regular form when I retire to rest at night, I rather sin than do anything that is good, unless my very soul speaks unto the Most High. Do you think that the King of heaven is delighted to hear you pronounce words with a frivolous tongue and a thoughtless mind? You know Him not. *"God is a Spirit: and they that worship Him must worship Him in spirit and in truth"* (John 4:24).

Beloved, the summary of all our remarks is just this: prayer is no trifle. It is an eminent and elevated act. It is a high and wondrous privilege. Under the old Persian Empire a few of the nobility were permitted at any time to come in to the king, and this was thought to be the highest privilege possessed by mortals. You and I, the people of God, have a permit, a passport, to come before the throne of heaven at any time we will, and we are encouraged to come there with great boldness. Still, let us not forget that it is no light thing to be a courtier in the courts of heaven and earth, to worship Him who made us and sustains us in being. Truly, when we attempt to pray, we may hear the voice saying out of the excellent glory, "Bow the knee." From all the spirits that behold the face of our Father who is in heaven, even now, I hear a voice that says,

O come, let us worship and bow down: let us kneel before the LORD *our maker. For he is our God; and we are the people of His pasture, and the sheep of His hand.*   (Psalm 95:6–7)

And, *"worship the* LORD *in the beauty of holiness. Fear before Him, all the earth"* (1 Chronicles 16:29–30).

GRACE

Lest the glow and brilliance of the word throne should be too much for mortal vision, our text now presents us with the soft, gentle radiance of that delightful word grace. We are called to the throne of grace, not to the throne of law. Rocky Sinai once was the throne of law when God came to Paran with ten thousand of His holy ones. (See Deuteronomy 33:2.) Who desired to draw near to that throne? Even Israel did not. Boundaries were set around the mount, and if even a beast touched the mount, it was stoned or thrust through with a dart. (See Hebrews 12:20.) Oh, selfrighteous ones who hope that you can obey the law and think that you can be saved by it, look to the flames that Moses saw, and shrink, and tremble, and despair. To that throne we do not come now, for through Jesus the case is changed. To a conscience purged by the precious blood, there is no anger upon the divine throne, though to our troubled minds:

> Once 'twas a seat of burning wrath,
> And shot devouring flame;
> Our God appeared consuming fire,
> And jealous was his name.

And, blessed be God, I am not now going to write about the throne of ultimate justice. Before that we will all come, and those of us who have believed will find it to be a throne of grace as well as of justice; for He who sits upon that throne will pronounce no sentence of condemnation against the man who is justified by faith. It is a throne set up on purpose for the dispensation of grace, a throne from which every utterance is an utterance of grace. The scepter that is stretched out from it is the silver scepter of grace. The decrees proclaimed from it are purposes of grace. The gifts that are scattered down its golden steps are gifts of grace. He who sits upon the throne is grace itself. It is *"the throne of grace"* to which we approach when we pray; let us think this over for a moment or two, by way of consolatory encouragement to those who are beginning to pray—indeed, to all of us who are praying men and women.

FAULTS OVERLOOKED

If in prayer I come before a throne of grace, then the many faults of my prayer will be overlooked. In beginning to pray, dear friends, you feel as if you did not pray. The groanings of your spirit, when you rise from your knees, are such that you think there is nothing in them. What a blotted, blurred, smeared prayer it is. Never mind. You have not come to the throne of justice, or else when God perceived the fault in the prayer, He would spurn it. Your broken words, your gaspings, your stammerings, are before a throne of grace.

OUR GRACIOUS KING DOES NOT MAINTAIN A STATELY ETIQUETTE IN HIS COURT LIKE THAT WHICH HAS BEEN OBSERVED BY PRINCES AMONG MEN, WHERE A LITTLE MISTAKE OR A FLAW WOULD SECURE THE PETITIONER'S BEING DISMISSED WITH DISGRACE. OH, NO. THE FAULTY CRIES OF HIS CHILDREN ARE NOT SEVERELY CRITICIZED BY HIM.

When any one of us has presented his best prayer before God, if he saw it as God sees it, there is no doubt he would make great lamentation over it. There is enough sin in the best prayer that was ever prayed to secure its being cast away from God. But it is not a throne of justice, I say again, and here is the hope for our lame, limping supplications. Our gracious King does not maintain a stately etiquette in His court like that which has been observed by princes among men, where a little mistake or a flaw would secure the petitioner's being dismissed with disgrace. Oh, no. The faulty cries of His children are not severely criticized by Him. The Lord High Chamberlain of the palace above, our Lord Jesus Christ, takes care to alter and amend every prayer before He presents it, and He makes the prayer perfect with His perfection and prevailing with His own merits. God looks upon the prayer as presented through Christ, and He forgives all of its own inherent faultiness.

How this ought to encourage any of us who feel ourselves to be feeble, wandering, and unskillful in prayer! If you cannot plead with God as sometimes you did in years gone by, if you feel as if somehow or other you have grown rusty in the work of supplication, never give up, but come still, yes, and come oftener. For it is not a throne of severe criticism; it is a throne of grace to which you come.

Then, further, inasmuch as it is a throne of grace, the faults of the petitioner himself will not prevent the success of his prayer. Oh, what faults there are in us! To come before a throne, how unfit we are—we, that are all defiled with sin within and without! Ah, I could not say to you, "Pray," not even to you saints, unless it were a throne of grace.

Much less could I talk of prayer to you sinners. But now I will say this to every sinner, though he thinks himself to be the worst sinner who ever lived: Cry to the Lord, and *"seek you the LORD while He may be found"* (Isaiah 55:6). A throne of grace is a place fitted for you; go to your knees. By simple faith go to the Savior, for He, He it is who is the throne of grace. It is in Him that God is able to dispense grace to the most guilty of mankind. Blessed be God, neither the faults of the prayer nor those of the suppliant will shut out our petitions from the God who delights in broken and contrite hearts.

DESIRES INTERPRETED

If it is a throne of grace, then the desires of the pleader will be interpreted. If I cannot find words in which to utter my desires, God in His grace will read my desires without the words. He takes the meaning of His saints, the meaning of their groans. A throne that was not gracious would not trouble itself to make out our petitions. But God, the infinitely gracious One, will dive into the soul of our desires, and He will read there what we cannot speak with the tongue.

Have you ever seen a parent, when his child is trying to say something to him and he knows very well what it is the little one has got to say, help him over the words and utter the syllables for him? If the little one has halfforgotten what he would say, you have seen the father suggest the word. Likewise, the everblessed Spirit, from the throne of grace, will help us and teach us words, no, write in our hearts the desires themselves. We have in Scripture instances where God puts words into sinners' mouths. "Take with you words," says He, "and say unto Him, 'Receive us graciously and love us freely.'" (See Hosea 14:2.)

He will put the desires and will put the expression of those desires into your spirit by His grace. He will direct your desires to the things for which you ought to seek. He will teach you your wants, though as yet you do not know them. He will suggest to you His promises so that you may be able to plead them. He will, in fact, be Alpha and Omega to your prayer just as He is to your salvation; for as salvation is from first to last of grace, so the sinner's approach to the throne of grace is of grace from first to last. What comfort this is. Will we not, my dear friends, with greater boldness draw near to this throne as we draw out the sweet meaning of these precious words, *"the throne of grace"*?

WANTS SUPPLIED

If it is a throne of grace, then all the wants of those who come to it will be supplied. The King on such a throne will not say, "You must bring to Me gifts; you must offer to Me sacrifices." It is not a throne for receiving tribute; it is a throne for dispensing gifts. Come, then, you that are poor as poverty itself. Come, you that have no merits and are destitute of virtues. Come, you that are reduced to a beggarly bankruptcy by Adam's fall and by your own transgressions. This is not the throne of majesty that supports itself by the taxation of its subjects, but it is a throne that glorifies itself by streaming forth like a fountain with floods of good things. Come, now, and receive the wine and milk that are freely given. *"Yea, come, buy wine and milk without money and without price"* (Isaiah 55:1). All the petitioner's wants will be supplied because it is a throne of grace.

"The throne of grace." The word grows as I turn it over in my mind. To me it is a most delightful reflection that if I come to the throne of God in prayer, I may see a thousand defects within me, but yet there is hope. I usually feel more dissatisfied with my prayers than with anything else I do. I do not believe that it is an easy thing to pray in public so as to

conduct the devotions of a large congregation rightly. We sometimes hear people commended for preaching well, but if any will be enabled to pray well, there will be an equal gift and a higher grace in it.

But, friends, suppose in our prayers there are defects of knowledge; it is a throne of grace, and our Father knows that we have need of these things. Suppose there are defects of faith; He sees our little faith and still does not reject it, small as it is. He does not in every case measure out His gifts by the degree of our faith, but by the sincerity and true-ness of faith. If there are grave defects in our spirit even, and failures in the fervency or in the humility of the prayer, still, though these should not be there and are much to be deplored, grace overlooks all this and forgives all this. Still, its merciful hand is stretched out to enrich us according to our needs. Surely this ought to induce many to pray who have not prayed, and this should make us who have long been accustomed to using the consecrated art of prayer, to draw near with greater boldness than ever to the throne of grace.

GRACE ENTHRONED

Now, regarding our text as a whole, it conveys to us the idea of grace enthroned. It is a throne, and who sits on it? It is Grace personified that is here installed in dignity. Truly, today, Grace is on a throne. In the gospel of Jesus Christ, grace is the most predominant attribute of God.

How does it come to be so exalted? Well, grace has a throne by conquest. Grace came down to earth in the form of the Well Beloved, and it met with sin. Long and sharp was the struggle, and grace appeared to be trampled underfoot by sin. But grace at last seized sin, threw it on its own shoulders, and, though all but crushed beneath the burden, grace carried sin up to the cross and nailed it there, slew it there, and put it to death forever. Grace triumphed gloriously. For this reason, grace sits on a throne at this hour because it has conquered human sin, has borne the penalty of human guilt, and has overthrown all its enemies.

Grace, moreover, sits on the throne because it has established itself there by right. There is no injustice in the grace of God. God is as just when He forgives a believer as when He casts a sinner into hell. I believe in my own soul that there is as much and as pure a justice in the acceptance of a soul who believes in Christ as there will be in the rejection of those souls who die impenitent and are banished from Jehovah's presence. The sacrifice of Christ has enabled God to *"be just, and [also] the justifier of him which believes in Jesus"* (Romans 3:26). He who knows the word *substitution* and can give its right meaning will see that there is nothing due to punitive justice from any believer, seeing that Jesus Christ has paid all the believer's debts. Now, God would be unjust if He did not save those for whom Christ vicariously suffered, for whom His righteousness was provided, and to whom it is imputed. Grace is on the throne by conquest, and it sits there by right.

Grace is enthroned this day, friends, because Christ has finished His work and has gone into the heavens. It is enthroned in power. When we speak of its throne, we mean that it has unlimited might. Grace sits not on the footstool of God, grace stands not in the courts of God, but it sits on the throne. It is the reigning attribute; it is the king today. This is the dispensation of grace, the year of grace; grace reigns through righteousness to eternal life. We live in the era of reigning grace. *"Seeing He ever lives to make intercession"* for the sons of men, Jesus *"is able also to save them to the uttermost that come to God by Him"* (Hebrews 7:25).

Sinner, if you were to meet grace in the byway, like a traveler on his journey, I would bid you to make its acquaintance and ask its influence. If you were to meet grace as a merchant on the exchange, with treasure in his hand, I would bid you to court its friendship; it would enrich you in the hour of poverty. If you were to see grace as one of the peers of heaven, highly exalted, I would bid you to seek to get its ear. But, oh, when grace sits on the throne, I beseech you, close in with it at once. It can be no higher; it can be no greater; for it is written, *"God is love"* (1 John 4:8), which is an alias for grace. Oh, come and bow before it; come and adore the infinite mercy and grace of God. Doubt not; halt not; hesitate not. Grace is reigning; grace is God; God is love. There is *"a rainbow round about the throne, in sight like to an emerald"* (Revelation 4:3), the emerald of His compassion and His love. Oh, happy are the souls who can believe this and, believing it, can come at once and glorify grace by becoming instances of its power.

THE GLORY OF GRACE

Lastly, our text, if rightly read, has in it sovereignty resplendent in glory—the glory of grace. The mercy seat is a throne; though grace is there, it is still a throne. Grace does not displace sovereignty. Now, the attribute of sovereignty is very high and terrible. Its light is like a jasper stone, most precious (see Revelation 21:11), and like a sapphire stone, or, as Ezekiel calls it, *"the terrible crystal"* (Ezekiel 1:22). Thus says the King, the Lord of Hosts, *"I will have mercy on whom I will have mercy, and I will have compassion on whom I will have compassion"* (Romans 9:15).

> *O man, who are you that replies against God? Shall the thing formed say to Him that formed it, Why have you made me thus? Has not the potter power over the clay, of the same lump to make one vessel to honor, and another to dishonor?* (Romans 9:20–21)

But, ah, lest any of you should be downcast by the thought of His sovereignty, I invite you to the text. It is a throne—there is sovereignty—but to every soul who knows how to pray, to every soul who by faith comes to Jesus, the true mercy seat, divine sovereignty wears no dark and terrible aspect but is full of love. It is a throne of grace. From this I gather that the sovereignty of God to a believer, to a pleader, to one who comes to God in Christ, is always exercised in pure grace. To you, to you who come to God in prayer, the sovereignty always goes like this: "I will have mercy on that sinner, though he does not deserve it, though in him there is no merit; yet because I can do as I will with My own, I will bless him, I will make him My child, and I will accept him. He will be Mine in the day when I make up My jewels."

There are yet two or three things to be discussed, and I will be done with this subject. On the throne of grace, sovereignty has placed itself under bonds of love. God will do as He wills; but, on the mercy seat, He is under bonds—bonds of His own making—for He has entered into covenant with Christ and so into covenant with His chosen. Though God is and ever must be a sovereign, He will never break His covenant, nor will He alter the word that is gone out of His mouth. He cannot be false to a covenant of His own making. When I come to God in Christ, to God on the mercy seat, I need not imagine that by any act of sovereignty God will set aside His covenant. That cannot be; it is impossible.

Moreover, on the throne of grace, God is again bound to us by His promises. The covenant contains in it many gracious promises, exceedingly great and precious. *"Ask, and it shall be given you; seek, and you shall find; knock, and it shall be opened to you"* (Matthew 7:7). Until God had said that word or a word to that effect, it was at His own option to hear prayer or not, but it is not so now. For now, if it is true prayer offered through Jesus Christ, His truth binds Him to hear it. A man may be perfectly free, but the moment he makes a promise, he is not free to break it; and the everlasting God does not want to break His promise. He delights to fulfill it. He has declared that all His promises are *"yes"* and *"amen"* (2 Corinthians 1:20) in Christ Jesus. For our consolation, when we survey God under the high and awesome aspect of His sovereignty, we have this to reflect on: He is under covenant bonds of promise to be faithful to the souls whoseek Him. His throne must be a throne of grace to His people.

Once more, and the sweetest thought of all, every covenant promise has been endorsed and sealed with blood, and far be it from the everlasting God to pour scorn upon the blood of His dear Son. When a king has given a charter to a city, he may have been absolute before, and there may have been nothing to check his prerogatives; however, when the city has its charter, then it pleads its rights before the king.

Even thus, God has given to His people a charter of untold blessings, bestowing upon them the sure mercies of David. Very much of the validity of a charter depends on the signature and the seal, and, my friends, how sure is the charter of covenant grace! The signature is the handwriting of God Himself, and the seal is the blood of the Only Begotten. The covenant is ratified with blood, the blood of His own dear Son. It is not possible that we can plead in vain with God when we plead the bloodsealed covenant, ordered in all things and sure. *"Heaven and earth shall pass away"* (Matthew 24:35), but the power of the blood of Jesus can never fail with God. It speaks when we are silent, and it prevails when we are defeated. *"Better things than that of Abel"* (Hebrews 12:24) does it ask for, and its cry is heard. Let us come boldly, for we bear the promise in our hearts. When we feel alarmed because of the sovereignty of God, let us cheerfully sing:

> The gospel bears my spirit up,
> A faithful and unchanging God
> Lays the foundation for my hope
> In oaths, and promises, and blood.

May God the Holy Spirit help us to use rightly from this time forward *"the throne of grace."* Amen.

3

THE SPIRIT OF PRAYER

Charles Finney

*Likewise the Spirit also helps our infirmities: for we know not what
we should pray for as we ought: but the Spirit Itself makes intercession for us with groanings which cannot be uttered. And He that
searches the hearts knows what is the mind of the Spirit, because He
makes intercession for the saints according to the will of God.*

(Romans 8:26–27)

We are ignorant of both the will of God as revealed in the Bible
and the unrevealed will of God as we can learn it from His providence. Mankind is also vastly ignorant of the promises and prophesies
in the Bible. We are even more in the dark about those points God gives
us through the leadings of His Spirit.

I have named these four reasons to ground our faith in prayer: providences, promises, prophecies, and the Holy Spirit. When all other
means fail to lead us to pray for the right things, the Spirit does it.

I once knew an individual who was in great spiritual darkness. He went off by himself to pray, resolving that he would not stop until he found the Lord. This man knelt down and tried to pray. His mind was dark, and he could not pray. He got up from his knees and stood awhile, but he could not give up because he had promised he would not let the sun go down before he gave himself to God. He knelt again, but his heart was as dark and hard as before. He was nearly in despair, and he said in agony, "I have grieved the Spirit of God away, and there is no hope for me. I am shut out from the presence of God."

HOW TO FIND HIM

But he was resolved not to give up. Again he knelt down. He had said only a few words when this passage came to mind, as fresh as if he had just read it: *"You shall seek Me, and find Me, when you shall search for Me with all your heart"* (Jeremiah 29:13). He saw that though this promise was in the Old Testament, and addressed to the Jews, it was as applicable to him as to them. His hard heart broke when the Lord Himself hammered it with this Scripture. This young man prayed and then got up to leave, filled with the joy of Jesus.[1]

INTERCESSORY PRAYER

I was acquainted with a pastor who used to keep a list of people for whom he was especially concerned, and I have had the opportunity to

---

1. In this passage, Finney uses the Pauline expression, *"I knew a man"* (2 Corinthians 12:2) to tell the story of his own conversion. It occurred at Adams, New York, where he was studying law. In his study of the Bible, he had come under deepening conviction, realizing that "salvation, instead of being a thing to be brought about by my own works, was a thing to be found entirely in the Lord Jesus, who presented Himself as my God and my Savior." As he walked along the street, an inward voice seemed to demand, "Will you accept it now, today?" His reply was, "Yes, I will accept it today, or I will die trying." Instead of going on to his studies, he made his way into the woods near the village and crept between some fallen trees to pray. There, as he said afterward, "God gave me many other promises in addition to the text quoted from Jeremiah, especially some very precious promises regarding our Lord Jesus Christ. I seized them." His disquieted mind became "wonderfully calm and peaceful." He thought, as he walked back toward Adams, "My mind was so perfectly quiet that it seemed as if all nature listened." He had gone to the woods immediately after an early breakfast, and by this time it was dinnertime. Yet it appeared to him that he had been absent only a little while. —E. E. Shelhamer [See Finney's *Holy Spirit Revivals* (New Kensington, PA: Whitaker House, 1999).]

know a multitude of people who were immediately converted after he began praying for them. I have seen him pray literally in agony for the people on this list. At times he would call on another Christian to help him pray for someone. His mind would become intensely fixed in prayer upon an individual who had a hardened, abandoned character, and who could not be reached in any ordinary way.

In one town where there was a revival, there was an individual who violently opposed Christianity. He ran a tavern and delighted in swearing whenever there were Christians within hearing distance. He was so bad that one man said he would either have to sell his place or give it away because he could not stand to live near a man who swore like that.

When this praying pastor passed through the town and heard of the case, he was very distressed for the individual, and he put the curser on his prayer list. The case weighed on his mind when he was asleep as well as when he was awake. He continued thinking about the ungodly man and praying for him for days. Not long afterward, the tavern keeper came to a meeting and confessed his sins. He poured out his soul, and he seemed to be one of the most repentant men ever seen. His testimony seemed to cover the whole ground of his treatment of God, Christians, the revival, and everything good. This new convert's bar immediately became the place where they held prayer meetings.[2]

The Spirit of God leads individual Christians to pray in this manner for things that they would not pray for without being led by the Spirit. In this way, they pray for things *according to the will of God* (Romans 8:27).

THE LEADING OF THE SPIRIT

A lot of harm has been done by those who say that this leading by the Spirit is a new revelation. Calling this leading a revelation has caused many people to be apprehensive of it. The strength of the term

---

2. In remarkable contrast, there was the case of a railing infidel who, in the middle of his discourse, suffered a stroke. A physician assured him that he did not have long to live, and that if he had anything to say, he must say it at once. He had only time and strength to stammer out one sentence. It was, "Don't let Finney pray over my corpse." —E. E. Shelhamer

has frightened them so that they will not even stop to see what revelation means or if the Bible even teaches the principle.

The plain truth of the matter is that the Spirit leads a man to pray. If God leads a man to pray for an individual, the inference from the Bible is that God plans to save that individual. If we find, by comparing our state of mind with the Bible, that we are led by the Spirit to pray for an individual, we have solid evidence to believe that God is prepared to bless him. Devoted, praying Christians often see these things so clearly, and look so far ahead, that they confuse others. They sometimes almost seem to prophesy.

Undoubtedly, many people think they are being led by the Spirit when in fact they are leaning on their own understanding. But there is no doubt that a Christian may be enabled to clearly discern the signs of the times so as to understand, by providence, what to expect, and to pray for it in faith. Believers are often led to expect a revival and to pray for it in faith, when nobody else can see the least sign of it.

UNDERSTANDING GOD'S DIRECTION

There was a woman living in a New Jersey town where there had just been a revival. She was positive there was going to be another. She wanted to arrange conference meetings, but the minister and elders saw nothing to encourage a revival, so they did nothing. She saw they were blind, so she got a carpenter to make seats for her house where she would have the meetings. There was certainly going to be a revival!

She had scarcely opened her doors for meetings when the Spirit of God came down with great power, and these sleepy Christians found themselves surrounded, all at once, with convicted sinners. They could only say, "*Surely the* LORD *is in this place; and* [we] *knew it not*" (Genesis 28:16).

People like this woman understand the direction of God's will because the Spirit of God leads them to the understanding, not because they are so wise. The Lord's wisdom shows them how events are all leading to a particular result.

As the Scripture text at the beginning of this chapter says, "*The Spirit Itself makes intercession for us with groanings which cannot be uttered.*" The meaning of this, as I understand it, is that the Spirit excites desires too great to be uttered except by groans—making the soul too full to utter its feelings by words. The person can only groan them out to God, who understands the language of the heart.

How is a sinner to get conviction? By thinking of his sins. That is also the way for a Christian to gain a deep awareness—by thinking about the subject. God is not going to pour these things on you without any effort of your own. You must cherish the slightest impressions. Take the Bible and go over the passages that show the conditions and prospects of the world. Look at the world, your children, and your neighbors and see their condition while they remain in sin. Then, persevere in prayer and effort until you obtain the blessing of the Spirit of God.

TAKE THE BIBLE AND GO OVER THE PASSAGES THAT SHOW THE CONDITIONS AND PROSPECTS OF THE WORLD. LOOK AT THE WORLD, YOUR CHILDREN, AND YOUR NEIGHBORS AND SEE THEIR CONDITION WHILE THEY REMAIN IN SIN. THEN, PERSEVERE IN PRAYER AND EFFORT UNTIL YOU OBTAIN THE BLESSING OF THE SPIRIT OF GOD.

I have spent much time on this subject because I want it to be plain to you so that you will be careful not to grieve the Spirit. I want you to have high ideas of the Holy Spirit and to recognize that nothing good will be done without His influences. No praying or preaching will make any difference without Him. If Jesus Christ were to come down here and preach to sinners, not one would be converted without the Spirit. Be careful, then, not to grieve Him by slighting or neglecting His heavenly influences when He invites you to pray.

PRAYER FORMS

We see from this subject the absurdity of using set prayers or prayer books. The very idea of using a form rejects the leading of the Spirit. Nothing is more calculated to destroy the spirit of prayer, and entirely darken and confuse the mind to what constitutes prayer, than prayer forms. Rote prayers are not only absurd in themselves, but they are the very device of the devil to destroy the spirit and break the power of prayer.

Prayer does not consist of mere words. It does not matter what the words are if the heart is not led by the Spirit of God. If the desire is not kindled, the thoughts directed, and the whole current of feeling produced and led by the Spirit of God, it is not prayer. Set forms keep an individual from praying as he could.

EXPERIENCING THE SPIRIT OF PRAYER

"The Spirit Itself makes intercession." For whom does He pray? For the saints! If you are a believer, you know by experience what it is to be exercised like this. Or, if you do not, it is because you have grieved the Spirit of God so that He will not lead you. You probably have not yet experienced His filling. You live in such a manner that this holy Comforter will not make His presence known with you or give you the spirit of prayer.

If this is so, you must repent. Do not stop to decide whether you are a Christian or not, but repent as if you have never repented. Do not take it for granted that you are a Christian, but go like a humble sinner and pour out your heart to the Lord. You can never have the spirit of prayer in any other way. Nothing will produce more excitement and opposition than the spirit of prayer.

4

TALKING TO GOD FOR MEN

E. M. Bounds

Let us often look at Brainerd, an American missionary to the native Indians, in the woods of America, pouring out his very soul before God for the perishing heathen without whose salvation nothing could make him happy. Prayer—secret, fervent, believing prayer—lies at the root of all personal godliness. A competent knowledge of the language where a missionary lives, a mild and winning temper, a heart given up to God in close religion—these, these are the attainments that, more than all knowledge or all other gifts, will fit us to become the instruments of God in the great work of human redemption.

—Carey's Brotherhood

There are two extreme tendencies in the ministry. The one is to shut itself out from fellowship with the people. The monk and the hermit are illustrations of this. They shut themselves out from men to be more with God. They failed, of course. Our being with God is of use only as we expend its priceless benefits on men.

Too often Christian leaders shut themselves in their studies and become students—bookworms, Bible experts, and sermon makers. They are noted for literature, thought, and sermons; but the people and God, where are they? Out of heart, out of mind. Preachers who are great thinkers, great students, must be the greatest of pray-ers. If they are not, they will be the greatest of backsliders, heartless professionals, rationalistic, less than the least of preachers in God's estimate.

The other tendency is to popularize the ministry thoroughly. It is no longer God's, but a ministry of affairs, of the people. The minister does not pray because his mission is to the people. If he can move the people, create a sensation in favor of religion, and an interest in church work, he is satisfied. His personal relationship to God is no factor in his work. Prayer has little or no place in his plans. The disaster and ruin of such a ministry cannot be computed by earthly mathematics. What the preacher is in prayer to God—for himself, for his people—so is his power for real good to men, his true fruitfulness, and his true fidelity to God—for time and for eternity.

It is impossible for the preacher to keep his spirit in harmony with the divine nature of his high calling without much and constant prayer. It is a serious mistake to think that the preacher, by duty and laborious fidelity to the work and routine of the ministry, can keep himself trim and fit for his high calling. Even sermon making—incessant and taxing as an art, as a duty, as a work, or as a pleasure—will engross, harden, and estrange the heart from God by neglect of prayer. The scientist loses God in nature. The preacher may lose God in his sermon.

Prayer freshens the heart of the preacher, keeps it in tune with God and in sympathy with the people. It lifts his ministry out of the chilly air of a profession, revitalizes routine, and moves every wheel with the ease and power of a divine anointing.

Charles Spurgeon has said,

Of course the preacher is above all others distinguished as a man of prayer. He prays as an ordinary Christian, else he were a hypocrite. He prays more than ordinary Christians, else he were disqualified for the office he has undertaken. If you as ministers are not very prayerful, you are to be pitied. If you become lax in sacred devotion, not only will you need to be pitied, but your people also, and the day approaches in which you will be ashamed and confounded. All our libraries and studies are mere emptiness compared with our prayer closets. Our seasons of fasting and prayer at the tabernacle have been high days indeed; never has heaven's gate stood wider; never have our hearts been nearer the central glory.

The praying that makes a prayerful ministry is not the meager praying added only as flavoring to give it a pleasant taste. But the praying must be in the body, form, blood, and bones. Prayer is no petty duty put into a corner. It is no piecemeal performance made out of the fragments of time that have been snatched from business and other engagements of life. The best of our time, and the heart of our time and strength, must be given to prayer. This does not mean that the closet is absorbed in the study or swallowed up in the activities of ministerial duties. But it means the closet first, the study and activities second. In this way, both the study and the activities are freshened and made efficient by the closet.

Prayer that affects one's ministry must touch one's life. The praying that gives color and bent to character is no pleasant, hurried pastime. It must enter as strongly into the heart and life as Christ's *"strong crying and tears"* (Hebrews 5:7) did. It must draw the soul into an agony of desire as Paul's did. It must be an in-wrought fire and force like the *"effectual fervent prayer"* (James 5:16) of James. The praying must be of that quality that, when put into the golden censer and incensed before God, works mighty, spiritual struggles and revolutions.

Prayer is not a little habit pinned onto us while we were tied to our mother's apron strings. Neither is it a little, decent quarter-of-a-minute's grace said over an hour's dinner. But it is a most serious work of our most serious years. It engages more of time and appetite than our longest dinings or richest feasts. The prayer that makes much of our preaching must itself be made much of. The character of our praying will determine the character of our preaching. Light praying will make light preaching. Prayer makes preaching strong, gives it an anointing, and makes it stick. In every ministry that is righteously working for good, prayer has always been a serious business.

THE PRAYER THAT MAKES MUCH OF OUR PREACHING MUST ITSELF BE MADE MUCH OF. THE CHARACTER OF OUR PRAYING WILL DETERMINE THE CHARACTER OF OUR PREACHING. LIGHT PRAYING WILL MAKE LIGHT PREACHING. PRAYER MAKES PREACHING STRONG, GIVES IT AN ANOINTING, AND MAKES IT STICK.

The preacher must primarily be a man of prayer. In the school of prayer, only the heart can learn to preach. No learning can make up for the failure to pray. No earnestness, no diligence, no study, no gifts will supply its lack.

Talking to men for God is a great thing, but talking to God for men is still greater. He who has not learned well how to talk to God for men will never talk well—with real success—to men for God. More than this, prayerless words, both in and out of the pulpit, are deadening.

5

THE FIGHT AGAINST PRAYERLESSNESS

Andrew Murray

As soon as the Christian becomes convinced of his sin in this matter, his first thought is that he must begin to strive, with God's help, to gain the victory over it. But alas, he soon experiences that his striving is worth little, and the discouraging thought comes over him, like a wave, that such a life is not for him—he cannot continue faithfully! At conferences on the subject of prayer, held during the past years, many a minister has openly said that it seemed impossible for him to attain such a strict life.

Recently, I received a letter from a minister, well-known for his ability and devotion, in which he wrote: "As far as I am concerned, it does not seem to help me to hear too much about the life of prayer, about the strenuous exertion for which we must prepare ourselves, and about all the time and trouble and endless effort it will cost us. These things discourage me; I have heard them so often. I have time after time put them to the test, and the result has always been sadly disappointing. It does not help me to be told: 'You must pray more, and hold a closer watch over yourself, and become altogether a more earnest Christian.'"

My reply to him was as follows: "I think in all I spoke at the conference or elsewhere, I have never mentioned exertion or struggle, because I am so entirely convinced that our efforts are futile unless we first learn how to abide in Christ by a simple faith."

My correspondent said further: "The message I need is this: 'See that your relationship to your living Savior is what it ought to be. Live in His presence, rejoice in His love, rest in Him.'"

A better message could not be given, if only it is rightly understood. "See that your relationship to the living Savior is what it ought to be." But this is just what will certainly make it possible for one to live the life of prayer.

We must not comfort ourselves with the thought of standing in a right relationship to the Lord Jesus while the sin of prayerlessness has power over us, and while we, along with the whole church, have to complain about our feeble lives that make us unfit to pray for ourselves, the church, or missions as we ought. But if we recognize that a right relationship to the Lord includes prayer, with both the desire and power to pray according to God's will, then we have something that gives us the right to rejoice in Him and to rest in Him.

I have related this incident to point out how discouragement will naturally be the result of self-effort and will shut out all hope of improvement or victory. And this indeed is the condition of many Christians when called on to persevere in prayer as intercessors. They feel it is something entirely beyond their reach. They believe that they do not have the power for the self-sacrifice and consecration necessary for such prayer. They shrink from the effort and struggle that will, as they suppose, make them unhappy. They have tried in the power of the flesh to conquer the flesh—a wholly impossible thing. They have endeavored by Beelzebub to cast out Beelzebub—this can never happen. It is Jesus alone who can subdue the flesh and the devil.

We have spoken of a struggle that will certainly result in disappointment and discouragement. This is the effort made in our own strength. But there is another struggle that will certainly lead to victory. The Scripture speaks of *"the good fight of faith"* (1 Timothy 6:12), that is to say, a fight that springs from and is carried on by faith. We must get right conceptions about faith and stand fast in our faith. Jesus Christ is always the Author and Finisher of our faith. (See Hebrews 12:2.) It is when we come into right relationship with Him that we can be sure of the help and power He bestows. Just as earnestly as we must, in the first place, say, "Do not strive in your own strength; cast yourself at the feet of the Lord Jesus, and wait upon Him in the sure confidence that He is with you and works in you"; so do we, in the second place, say, "Strive in prayer; let faith fill your heart; so will you be strong in the Lord and in the power of His might."

An illustration will help us to understand this. A devoted Christian woman who conducted a large Bible class with zeal and success came to see her minister quite troubled. In her earlier years, she had enjoyed much blessing in the inner chamber, in fellowship with the Lord and His Word. But this had gradually been lost, and, do what she would, she could not get right. The Lord had blessed her work, but the joy had gone out of her life. The minister asked what she had done to regain the lost blessedness. "I have done everything," said she, "that I can think of, but all in vain."

He then questioned her about her experience in connection with her conversion. She gave an immediate and clear answer: "At first I spared no pains in my attempt to become better and to free myself from sin, but it was all useless. At last I began to understand that I must lay aside all my efforts, and simply trust the Lord Jesus to bestow on me His life and peace, and He did it."

"Why then," said the minister, "do you not try this again? As you go to your inner chamber, however cold and dark your heart may be, do not try in your own might to force yourself into the right attitude. Bow before Him, and tell Him that He sees in what a sad state you are and that your only hope is in Him. Trust Him with a childlike trust to have mercy upon you, and wait upon Him. In such a trust you are in a right relationship to Him. You have nothing; He has everything." Some time later she told the minister that his advice had helped her. She had learned that faith in the love of the Lord Jesus is the only method of getting into fellowship with God in prayer.

Do you begin to see, my reader, that there are two kinds of warfare—the first when we seek to conquer prayerlessness in our own strength? In that case, my advice to you is: "Give over your restlessness and effort; fall helpless at the feet of the Lord Jesus. He will speak the word, and your soul will live." If you have done this, then, second, comes the message: "This is but the beginning of everything. It will require deep earnestness and the exercise of all your power and a watchfulness of the entire heart—eager to detect the least backsliding. Above all, it will require a surrender to a life of self-sacrifice that God really desires to see in us and which He will work out for us."

6

UNDER THE BLOOD

Charles Spurgeon

Jehovah, our God, we thank You for leaving on record the story of Your ancient people. It is full of instruction to us. Help us to take its warning to avoid the faults into which they fell! You are a covenant God, and You keep Your promises. Your Word never fails. We have proved this to be so:

> Thus far we find that promise good,
> Which Jesus ratified with blood.

Nonetheless, as for ourselves, we are like Israel of old, a fickle people. We confess with great shame that although there are days when we take the tambourine and sing with Moses *"to the LORD, for He has triumphed gloriously"* (Exodus 15:1), yet, not many hours later, we are thirsty, we cry for water, and we murmur in our tents. Bitter Marah turns our hearts (see verses 22–25), and we are grieved with You, our God. When we behold Your Sinai covered in smoke, we bow before You with reverence and awe, but there have been times when we have set up the golden calf and have said of some earthly thing, *"These be your gods, O Israel"* (Exodus 32:4). We believe with intensity of faith and then doubt with a horribleness of doubt.

Lord, You have been very patient with us. Many have been our provocations, many have been Your chastisements, but Your strokes are fewer than our crimes, And lighter than our guilt. You have *"not dealt with us after our sins; nor rewarded us according to our iniquities"* (Psalm 103:10). Blessed be Your name! And now fulfill that part of the covenant wherein You have said, *"A new heart also will I give you, and a new Spirit will I put within you"* (Ezekiel 36:26). *"I will put My fear in their hearts, that they shall not depart from Me"* (Jeremiah 32:40). Hold us fast, and then we will hold fast to You. Turn us, and we will be turned. Keep us, and we will keep Your statutes.

We cry to You that we may no longer provoke You. We beg You to send the serpents among us rather than to let sin come among us. Oh, that we might have our eyes always on the bronze serpent that heals all the bites of evil (see Numbers 21:9), but may we not look to sin or love it. Do not let the devices of Balaam and of Balak prevail against us, to lead Your people away from their purity. Do not let us be defiled with false doctrine or with unholy living, but may we walk as the separated people of God and keep ourselves unspotted from the world. Lord, we do not want to grieve Your Spirit. May we never vex You so as to lead You in Your wrath to say, *"They shall not enter into My rest"* (Hebrews 3:11). Bear with us still for the dear sake of Him whose blood is upon us. Bear with us still. Do not send the destroying angel as You did to Egypt, but again fulfill that promise of Yours: *"When I see the blood, I will pass over you"* (Exodus 12:13).

Just now may we be consciously passed over by the Spirit of condemnation. May we know in our hearts that *"there is therefore now no condemnation to them which are in Christ Jesus"* (Romans 8:1). May we feel the peace-giving power of divine absolution. May we come into Your holy presence with our feet washed in the bronze laver, hearing our Great High Priest say to us, "[You are] *clean every whit"* (John 13:10).

Thus made clean, may we draw near to God through Jesus Christ our Lord.

Further, our heavenly Father, we come before You now washed in the blood, wearing the snowy-white robe of Christ's righteousness, and we ask You to remember Your people. Some are sorely burdened. Lighten the burden or strengthen the shoulder. Some are bowed down with fear, and perhaps they mistrust You. Forgive the mistrust, and give a great increase of faith so that they may trust You where they cannot trace You. Lord, remember any who bear the burdens of others. Some cry to You day and night about the sins of the times, about the wanderings of Your church. Lord, hear our prayers! We want to bear this yoke for You, but help us to bear it without the fear that causes us to distrust You. May we know that You will take care of Your own case and preserve Your own truth, and may we thus be restful about it all.

Some are crying to You for the conversion of relatives and friends. They have taken up this burden to follow after Jesus in the matter of cross bearing. Grant them to see the desire of their hearts fulfilled. God, save our children and our children's children, and if we have unconverted relatives of any kind, Lord, have mercy on them for Christ's sake. Give us joy in them—as much joy in them as Christians as we have had sorrow about them as unbelievers.

Further, be pleased to visit Your church with the Holy Spirit. Renew the day of Pentecost in our midst. In the midst of all gatherings of Your people, may there come the descension of the holy fire, the uprising of the heavenly wind. May matters that are now slow and dead become quick and full of life, and may the Lord Jesus Christ be exalted in the midst of His church, which is His fullness, *"the fullness of Him that fills all in all"* (Ephesians 1:23). May multitudes be converted. May they come flocking to Christ with holy eagerness to find in Him a refuge, even as the doves fly to their dovecotes.

Oh, for salvation work throughout these islands, across the sea, and in every part of the world, especially in heathen lands. Bring many to Christ's feet, we pray, everywhere that men are ready to lay down their lives to impart the heavenly life of Christ. Lord, work mightily! Your church cries to You, "Do not leave us. We can do nothing without You!" Our strength is wholly Yours. Come to us with great power, and let Your Word have free course and be glorified.

Remember everyone who calls You Father. May Your Father's love look on all the children. May the special need of each one be supplied, the special sorrow of each one be eased. May we be growing Christians; may we be working Christians; may we be perfected Christians; may we come to *"to the measure of the stature of the fullness of Christ"* (Ephesians 4:13). Lord Jesus, You are a great pillar. In You all fullness dwells. (See Colossians 1:19.) You began Your ministry with filling the waterpots full. You filled Simon Peter's boat until it began to sink. You filled the house where Your people met together with the presence of the Holy Spirit. You fill heaven. You will surely fill all things. Fill us; oh, fill us today with all the fullness of God! Thus make Your people joyful, strong, gracious, and heavenly!

But we cannot end our prayer when we have prayed for just Your people, though we have asked large things. We want You to look among the thousands and millions all around us who do not know You. Lord, look on the masses who go nowhere to worship. Have pity on them. *"Father, forgive them; for they know not what they do"* (Luke 23:34). Give them a desire to hear Your Word. Send the people a desire for their God.

O Lord, take sinners in hand Yourself. Come and reach obstinate, hardened minds. Let the careless and the frivolous begin to think about eternal things. May there be an uneasiness of heart, a sticking of the arrows of God in their bodies. May they seek the Great Physician and find healing this very day. Lord, You say, *"To day if you will hear [My] voice, harden not your heart"* (Psalm 95:7–8), and we take up the echo. Save men today, even today. Bring them Your Spirit in power so that they may be willing to rest in Christ. Lord, hear, forgive, accept, and bless for Jesus's sake. Amen.

7

CONDITIONS OF PREVAILING PRAYER

George Müller

DEPEND ON JESUS

The first condition of prevailing prayer is an entire dependence upon the merits and mediation of the Lord Jesus Christ as the only ground of any claim for blessing. Consider the following verses:

And whatsoever you shall ask in My name, that will I do, that the Father may be glorified in the Son. If you shall ask anything in My name, I will do it. (John 14:13–14)

You have not chosen Me, but I have chosen you, and ordained you, that you should go and bring forth fruit, and that your fruit should remain: that whatsoever you shall ask of the Father in My name, He may give it you. (John 15:16)

FORSAKE SIN

Second, there must be a separation from all known sin. God will not sanction sin. The Scripture says,

> *If I regard iniquity in my heart, the Lord will not hear me.*
> (Psalm 66:18)

EXERCISE FAITH

Third, one must exercise faith in God's Word of promise as confirmed by His oath. Not to believe Him is to make Him out to be both a liar and a perjurer.

> *For when God made promise to Abraham, because He could swear by no greater, He swore by Himself, saying, Surely blessing I will bless you, and multiplying I will multiply you. And so, after he had patiently endured, he obtained the promise. For men verily swear by the greater: and an oath for confirmation is to them an end of all strife. Wherein God, willing more abundantly to show to the heirs of promise the immutability of His counsel, confirmed it by an oath: that by two immutable things, in which it was impossible for God to lie, we might have a strong consolation, who have fled for refuge to lay hold upon the hope set before us: which hope we have as an anchor of the soul, both sure and steadfast, and which enters into that inside the veil; where the forerunner is for us entered, even Jesus, made a high priest for ever after to the order of Melchisedec.*
> (Hebrews 6:13–20)

> *But without faith it is impossible to please Him: for he that comes to God must believe that He is, and that He is a rewarder of them that diligently seek Him.*   (Hebrews 11:6)

> *He that says, I know Him, and keeps not His commandments, is a liar, and the truth is not in him.*   (1 John 2:4)

ASK ACCORDING TO HIS WILL

Fourth, ask in accordance with His will. Our motives must be godly. We must not seek any gift of God for selfish purposes.

And this is the confidence that we have in Him, that, if we ask any thing according to His will, He hears us.   (1 John 5:14)

You ask, and receive not, because you ask amiss, that you may consume it upon your lusts.   (James 4:3)

PERSEVERE IN PRAYER

Fifth, there must be perseverance in prayer. There must be a waiting on God and a waiting for God, as the farmer has long patience to wait for the harvest.

And He spoke a parable to them to this end, that men always ought to pray, and not to faint; saying, There was in a city a judge, which feared not God, neither regarded man: and there was a widow in that city; and she came to him, saying, Avenge me of mine adversary. And he would not for a while: but afterward he said within himself, Though I fear not God, nor regard man; yet because this widow troubles me, I will avenge her, lest by her continual coming she weary me. And the Lord said, Hear what the unjust judge says. And shall not God avenge His own elect, which cry day and night to Him, though He bear long with them? I tell you that He will avenge them speedily. Nevertheless when the Son of Man comes, shall He find faith on the earth?   (Luke 18:1–8)

Be patient therefore, brethren, to the coming of the Lord. Behold, the husbandman waits for the precious fruit of the earth, and has long patience for it, until he receive the early and latter rain.

(James 5:7)

8

CONFESSION

D. L. Moody

Another element in true prayer is confession. I do not want Christian friends to think that I am talking to the unsaved. I think that, as Christians, we have many sins to confess.

If you go back to the Scripture records, you will find that the men who lived nearest to God and had the most power with Him were those who confessed their sins and failures. Daniel, as we have seen, confessed his sins and those of his people. (See Daniel 9:20.) Yet there is nothing recorded against Daniel. He was one of the best men on the face of the earth, yet his confession of sin was one of the deepest and most humble on record. Thomas Brooks, referring to Daniel's confession, said,

In these words [Daniel 9:5–6 KJV] you have seven circumstances that Daniel useth in confessing of his and the people's sins, and all to heighten and to aggravate them. First, "We have sinned"; secondly, "We have committed iniquity"; thirdly, "We have done wickedly"; fourthly, "We have rebelled against thee";

fifthly, "We have departed from thy precepts"; sixthly, "We have not hearkened unto thy servants"; seventhly, "Nor our princes, nor all the people of the land." These seven aggravations which Daniel reckons up in his confession, are worthy of our most serious consideration.[3]

Job was no doubt a holy man, a mighty prince, yet he had to fall in the dust and confess his sins. You will find the necessity of confession all through the Bible. When Isaiah saw the purity and holiness of God, he beheld himself in his true state and exclaimed, *"Woe is me! for I am undone; because I am a man of unclean lips"* (Isaiah 6:5).

I firmly believe that the church of God will have to confess her own sins before there can be any great work of grace. There must be a deeper work among God's believing people. I sometimes think it is about time to give up preaching to the ungodly and preach to those who profess to be Christians. If we had a higher standard of life in the church of God, there would be thousands more flocking into the kingdom. It was so in the past; when God's believing children turned away from their sins and their idols, the fear of God fell upon the people around them. Look at the history of Israel, and you will find that when they put away their strange gods, God visited the nation, and there came a mighty work of grace.

What we want in these days is a true, deep revival in the church of God. I have little sympathy with the idea that God is going to reach the masses by a cold, formal church. *"The time is come that judgment must begin at the house of God"* (1 Peter 4:17)—with us.

Notice that when Daniel got that wonderful answer to prayer recorded in the ninth chapter, he was confessing his sin. That is one of the best chapters on prayer in the whole Bible. We read,

And while I was speaking, and praying, and confessing my sin and the sin of my people Israel, and presenting my supplication before the

---

3. Thomas Brooks, *The Complete Works of Thomas Brooks*, Volume 3 (Edinburgh: John Greig and Son, 1866), 407.

LORD my God for the holy mountain of my God; yea, while I was
speaking in prayer, even the man Gabriel, whom I had seen in the
vision at the beginning, being caused to fly swiftly, touched me about
the time of the evening oblation. And he informed me, and talked
with me, and said, O Daniel, I am now come forth to give you skill
and understanding. (Daniel 9:20–22)

So, too, when Job was confessing his sin, God turned his captivity
and heard his prayer. God will hear our prayer and turn our captivity
when we take our true place before Him and confess and forsake our
transgressions. It was when Isaiah cried out before the Lord, *"I am un-*
done" (Isaiah 6:5), that the blessing came; the live coal was taken from
the altar and put upon his lips, and he went out to write one of the most
wonderful books the world has ever seen. What a blessing it has been
to the church!

It was when David said, *"I have sinned"* (2 Samuel 12:13), that God
dealt in mercy with him. He confessed his sin to God:

I acknowledged my sin to You, and my iniquity have I not hidden. I
said, I will confess my transgressions to the LORD; and You forgave
the iniquity of my sin. (Psalm 32:5)

Notice how David made a very similar confession to that of the
prodigal in the fifteenth chapter of Luke. These are the words of the
prodigal son:

And the son said to him, Father, I have sinned against heaven, and
in your sight, and am no more worthy to be called your son.
(Luke 15:21)

David's confession went as follows:

For I acknowledge my transgressions: and my sin is ever before me.
Against You, You only, have I sinned, and done this evil in Your
sight. (Psalm 51:3–4)

There is no difference between the king and the beggar when the Spirit of God comes into the heart and convicts of sin.

Richard Sibbes, a Puritan preacher, quaintly said of confession,

This is the way to give glory to God…. When we have laid open our souls to God, and laid as much against ourselves as the devil could do that way—for let us think what the devil would lay to our charge at the hour of death and the day of judgment, he would lay hard to our charge this and that—let us accuse ourselves as he would, and as he will ere long. The more we accuse and judge ourselves, and set up a tribunal in our hearts, certainly there will follow an incredible ease. Jonah was cast into the sea, and there was an ease in the ship; Achan was stoned, and the plague was stayed. Out with Jonah, out with Achan, and there will follow ease and quiet in the soul presently; conscience will receive wonderful ease. It must needs be so, for when God is honoured conscience is purified. God is honoured by confession of sin every way. It honours his omniscience; that he is all-seeing, that he sees our sins and searcheth the hearts. Our secrets are not hid from him. It honours his power. What makes us confess our sins, but that we are afraid of his power, lest he should execute it? And what makes us confess our sins, but that we know there is "mercy with him that he may be feared" (Psalm 130:4), and that there is pardon for sin? We would not confess our sins else. With men it is confess and have execution, but with God confess and have mercy. It is his own protestation. We should never lay open our sins but for mercy. So it honours God; and when he is honoured, he honours the soul with inward peace and tranquillity.[4]

Thomas Fuller, an English author and clergyman, said, "Man's owning his weakness is the only stock for God thereon to graft the grace of his assistance."[5]

---

4. Thomas Sibbes, *The Complete Works of Richard Sibbes* (Edinburgh: James Nichol, 1862).
5. Thomas Fuller, *The Wit and Wisdom of Thomas Fuller* (London, The Religious Tract Society, 1886), 106.

Confession implies humility, and humility, in God's sight, is of great price.

A farmer went with his son into a wheat field to see if it was ready for the harvest. "See, father," exclaimed the boy, "how straight these stems hold up their heads! They must be the best ones. Those that hang their heads down cannot be good for much, I am sure." The farmer plucked a stalk of each kind and said, "See here, foolish child! This stalk that stood so straight is light-headed and almost good for nothing, while this that hung its head so modestly is full of the most beautiful grain."

Outspokenness is necessary and powerful, both with God and man. We need to be honest and frank with ourselves. A soldier said in a revival meeting, "My fellow soldiers, I am not excited; I am *convinced*—that is all. I feel that I ought to be a Christian and that I ought to say so, to tell you so, and to ask you to come with me. Now, if there is a call for sinners seeking Christ to come forward, I for one shall go—not to make a show, for I have nothing but sin to show. I do not go because I want to—I would rather keep my seat—but going will be telling the truth. I ought to be a Christian, I want to be a Christian, and going forward for prayer is just telling the truth about it." More than twenty men went with him.

Speaking of Pharaoh's words, *"Entreat the* LORD, *that He may take away the frogs from me"* (Exodus 8:8), Charles Spurgeon said,

> A fatal flaw is manifest in that prayer. It contains no confession of sin. He says not, "I have rebelled against the Lord; entreat that I may find forgiveness!" Nothing of the kind: he loves sin as much as ever. A prayer without penitence is a prayer without acceptance. If no tear has fallen upon it, it is withered. Thou must come to God as a sinner through a Savior, but by no other way. He that comes to God like the Pharisee, with, "God, I thank thee that I am not like other men are," never draws near to God at all; but he that cries, "God be merciful to me a sinner," has come to God by the way which God has himself appointed. There must be a confession of sin before God, or our prayer is faulty.[6]

6. Charles H. Spurgeon, *The Complete Works of C. H. Spurgeon: Volume 59, Sermons 3335 to 3386* (Ft. Collins, CO: Delmarva Publications, 2013).

If this confession of sin is deep among believers, it will be so among the ungodly also. I have never known it to fail. I am now anxious for God to revive His work in the hearts of His children so that we may see the exceeding sinfulness of sin. There are many Christian fathers and mothers who are anxious for the conversion of their children. I have had as many as fifty messages from parents come to me within a single week, wondering why their children are not saved and asking prayer for them. I venture to say that, as a rule, the fault lies at our own doors. (See Genesis 4:7.) There may be something in our lives that stands in the way. It may be there is some secret sin that keeps back the blessing. David lived in his awful sin for many months before Nathan made his appearance. Let us ask God to come into our hearts and make His power felt. If it is a right eye that causes us to sin, let us pluck it out; if it is a right hand, let us cut it off (see Matthew 5:29–30), so that we may have power with God and with man.

Why is it that so many of our children are wandering off into the barrooms and drifting away into unbelief—going down to a dishonored grave? There seems to be very little power in the Christianity of the present time. Many godly parents find that their children are going astray. Does it arise from some secret sin clinging around the parents' hearts? There is a passage of God's Word that is often quoted, but in ninety-nine cases out of a hundred, those who quote it stop at the wrong place. In the fifty-ninth chapter of Isaiah we read, *"Behold, the* LORD's *hand is not shortened, that it cannot save; neither His ear heavy, that it cannot hear"* (verse 1). There they stop. Of course, God's hand is not shortened and His ear is not heavy, but we ought to read the next two verses:

> *But your iniquities have separated between you and your God, and your sins have hidden His face from you, that He will not hear. For your hands are defiled with blood, and your fingers with iniquity; your lips have spoken lies, your tongue has muttered perverseness.*
> (Isaiah 59:2–3)

As Matthew Henry said, "It was owing to themselves; they stood in their own light and put a bar in their own door. God was coming towards them in ways of mercy and they hindered him. 'Your iniquities have kept good things from you,' Jer. 5:25."[7]

Bear in mind that if we are regarding iniquity in our hearts or depending on an empty mouthing of our faith, we have no claim to expect that our prayers will be answered. (See Psalm 66:18.) There is not one solitary promise for us. I sometimes tremble when I hear people quote promises and say that God is bound to fulfill those promises to them, when all the time there is something in their own lives that they are not willing to give up. It is well for us to search our hearts and find out why it is that our prayers are not answered.

I SOMETIMES TREMBLE WHEN I HEAR PEOPLE QUOTE PROMISES AND SAY THAT GOD IS BOUND TO FULFILL THOSE PROMISES TO THEM, WHEN ALL THE TIME THERE IS SOMETHING IN THEIR OWN LIVES THAT THEY ARE NOT WILLING TO GIVE UP. IT IS WELL FOR US TO SEARCH OUR HEARTS AND FIND OUT WHY IT IS THAT OUR PRAYERS ARE NOT ANSWERED.

Let me quote a very solemn passage in Isaiah:

Hear the word of the LORD, you rulers of Sodom; give ear to the law of our God, you people of Gomorrah. To what purpose is the multitude of your sacrifices to Me? says the LORD: I am full of the burned offerings of rams, and the fat of fed beasts; and I delight not in the blood of bullocks, or of lambs, or of he goats. When you come to

---

7. Matthew Henry, *Matthew Henry's Commentary on the Whole Bible: Volume IV–I, Isaiah* (Woodstock, Ontario: Devoted Publishing, 2017), 328.

appear before Me, who has required this at your hand, to tread My
courts? Bring no more vain oblations; incense is an abomination to
Me; the new moons and sabbaths, the calling of assemblies, I cannot
away with; it is iniquity, even the solemn meeting.

(Isaiah 1:10–13)

"*The solemn meeting*"—think of that! If God does not get our heart
services, He will have none of our outward services; they are an abomination to Him.

Your new moons and your appointed feasts My soul hates: they are
a trouble to Me; I am weary to bear them. And when you spread
forth your hands, I will hide My eyes from you: yea, when you make
many prayers, I will not hear: your hands are full of blood. Wash
you, make you clean; put away the evil of your doings from before
My eyes; cease to do evil; learn to do well; seek judgment, relieve the
oppressed, judge the fatherless, plead for the widow. Come now, and
let us reason together, says the LORD: *though your sins be as scarlet,*
they shall be as white as snow; though they be red like crimson, they
shall be as wool.

(verses 14–18)

Again, we read in Proverbs: "*He that turns away his ear from hearing*
the law, even his prayer shall be an abomination" (Proverbs 28:9). Think
of that! It may shock some of us to think that our prayers are an abomination to God, yet if any are living in known sin, this is what God's
Word says about them. If we are not willing to turn from sin and obey
God's law, we have no right to expect that He will answer our prayers.
Unconfessed sin is unforgiven sin, and unforgiven sin is the darkest,
foulest thing on this sin-cursed earth. You cannot find a case in the Bible
where a man has been honest in dealing with sin and God has not been
honest with him and blessed him. The prayer of the humble, contrite
heart is a delight to God. There is no sound that goes up from this sin-
cursed earth that is so sweet to His ear as the prayer of the man who is
walking uprightly.

Let me call attention to that prayer of David, in which he said,

Search me, O God, and know my heart: try me, and know my thoughts: and see if there be any wicked way in me, and lead me in the way everlasting. (Psalm 139:23–24)

I wish all my readers would commit these verses to memory. If we would all honestly make this prayer once every day, there would be a good deal of change in our lives. "*Search me*"—not my neighbor. It is so easy to pray for other people but so hard to get honest with ourselves. I am afraid that we who are busy in the Lord's work are very often in danger of neglecting our own vineyards. In this psalm, David got honest about himself. There is a difference between God searching me and my searching myself. I may search my heart and pronounce it all right, but when God searches me with His light, a lot of things come to light that perhaps I knew nothing about.

"*Try me.*" David was tried when he fell by taking his eye off the God of his father Abraham. "*Know my thoughts.*" God looks at the thoughts. Are our thoughts pure? Do we have in our hearts thoughts against God or against His people— against anyone in the world? If we have, we are not right in the sight of God. Oh, may God search us, all of us! I do not know any better prayer that we can make than this prayer of David. One of the most solemn truths in biblical history is that when holy men—better people than we are—were tested and tried, they were found to be as weak as water away from God.

Let us be sure that we are right with God. Isaac Ambrose wrote the following pithy words:

Now and then propose we to our hearts these two questions: 1. Heart, how dost thou?" a few words, but a very serious question: you know, this is the first question, and the first salute that we use to one another, How do you Sir? I would to God we would sometimes thus speak to our hearts, Heart, how dost thou? how is it with thee for thy Spiritual estate? 2. Heart, what wilt thou do? or, Heart, what dost thou think will become of thee and me? as that dying Roman once said, Poor, wretched, miserable soul, whither art thou and I going, and what will become of thee, when thou and I shall part? This very thing does Moses propose to Israel, though in other terms, O that they would consider their latter ends! And O that we would propose this question constantly to our hearts, to consider and debate upon! Commune within your hearts, said David; that is, debate the matter betwixt you and your own hearts to the very utmost: let your hearts be so put to it in communing with them, as that they may speak their very bottom. Commune, or hold a serious communication, and clear intelligence and acquaintance with your own hearts.[8]

The following is the confession of a theologian, sensible of his neglect, and especially of the difficulty of this duty:

[QI]I have lived these forty years, and somewhat more, and carried my heart in my bosom all this while, and yet my heart and I are as great strangers and as utterly unacquainted, as if we had never come near one another....

I know not my heart, I have forgotten my heart. ...That I could be grieved at the very heart, that my poor heart and I have been so unacquainted! ...We are fallen into an Athenian age, as Acts 17:21; "spending our time in nothing more than in telling, or in hearing, news, or some new thing": how go things here, how there,—how in one place, how in another? But who is there that is inquisitive,—How are things with my poor heart?...

Weigh but in the balance of a serious consideration, what time you have spent otherwise, and what time you have spent in this,—and for many scores or hundreds of hours or days that you owe to your hearts in this duty, can you write "fifty?" Or

---

8. Isaac Ambrose, *Media: The Middle Things, in Reference to the First and Last Things* (1652), 66.

go to the heap of your whole life, and where there should have been twenty measures employed about this business, can you find ten? Or where there should have been fifty vessels full of this duty, can we find twenty?

...Days and years bestowed upon the affairs of the world and worldliness, months and weeks spent and laid out in converse with friends and strangers, but scarce a minute in converse with a man's own heart.[9]

If there is anything in our lives that is wrong, let us ask God to show it to us. Have we been selfish? Have we been more jealous of our own reputation than of the honor of God? Elijah thought he was very jealous for the honor of God, but it turned out that it was his own honor after all—self was really at the bottom of it.

One of the saddest things, I think, that Christ had to meet with in His disciples was this very thing; there was a constant struggle between them as to who should be the greatest, instead of each one taking the humblest place and being least in his own estimation.

We are told in proof of this, the following:

And He came to Capernaum: and being in the house He asked them, What was it that you disputed among yourselves by the way? But they held their peace: for by the way they had disputed among themselves, who should be the greatest. And He sat down, and called the twelve, and says to them, If any man desire to be first, the same shall be last of all, and servant of all. And He took a child, and set him in the midst of them: and when He had taken him in His arms, He said to them, Whosoever shall receive one of such children in My name, receives Me: and whosoever shall receive Me, receives not Me, but Him that sent Me. (Mark 9:33–37)

Soon after that, a similar incident occurred:

9. John Lightfoot, *The Whole Works of the Rev. John Lightfood, D.D.* (London: J. F. Dove, 1822), 112–114.

And James and John, the sons of Zebedee, come to Him, saying, Master, we would that You should do for us whatsoever we shall desire. And He said to them, What would you that I should do for you? They said to Him, Grant to us that we may sit, one on Your right hand, and the other on Your left hand, in Your glory. But Jesus said to them, You know not what you ask: can you drink of the cup that I drink of? and be baptized with the baptism that I am baptized with? And they said to Him, We can. And Jesus said to them, You shall indeed drink of the cup that I drink of; and with the baptism that I am baptized with shall you be baptized: but to sit on My right hand and on My left hand is not Mine to give; but it shall be given to them for whom it is prepared. And when the ten heard it, they began to be much displeased with James and John. But Jesus called them to Him, and says to them, You know that they which are accounted to rule over the Gentiles exercise lordship over them; and their great ones exercise authority upon them. But so shall it not be among you: but whosoever will be great among you, shall be your minister: and whosoever of you will be the chiefest, shall be servant of all. For even the Son of man came not to be ministered to, but to minister, and to give His life a ransom for many.   (Mark 10:35–45)

The latter words were spoken in the third year of His ministry. For three years the disciples had been with Him. They had listened to the words that fell from His lips, but they had failed to learn this lesson of humility. The most humiliating thing that happened among the Twelve occurred on the night of our Lord's betrayal, when Judas sold Him and Peter denied Him.

If there was any place where there should have been an absence of these thoughts about status and position, it was at the supper table. Yet, we find that when Christ instituted that blessed memorial there was a debate going on among His disciples about who would be the greatest. Think of that! Right before the cross, when the Master was *"exceeding sorrowful, even to death"* (Matthew 26:38); when He was already tasting the bitterness of Calvary, and the horrors of that dark hour were gathering upon His soul!

I think if God searches us, we will find a lot of things in our lives to confess. If we are tried and tested by God's law, there will be many things that will have to be changed. I ask again: Are we selfish or jealous? Are we willing to hear of others being used by God more than we are? Are the Methodists willing to hear of a great revival of God's Word among the Baptists? Would it rejoice their souls to hear of such efforts being blessed? Are Baptists willing to hear of a reviving of God's work in the Methodist, Congregational, or other churches? If we are full of narrow party and sectarian feelings, there will be many things to be laid aside. Let us pray to God to search us, try us, and see if there is any evil way in us. If these holy and good men felt that they were faulty, should we not tremble and endeavor to find out if there is anything in our lives that God would have us get rid of?

Once again, let me call your attention to the prayer of David contained in the fifty-first Psalm. A friend of mine told me some years ago that he repeated this prayer as his own every week. I think it would be a good thing if we offered up these petitions frequently; let them go right up from our hearts. If we have been proud or irritable or lacking in patience, should we not at once confess it? Is it not time that we begin at home and get our lives straightened out? See how quickly the ungodly will then begin to inquire about the way of life! Let those of us who are parents set our own houses in order and be filled with Christ's Spirit; then it will not be long before our children will be asking what they must do to get the same Spirit.

I believe that today, by its lukewarmness and formality, the Christian church is making more infidels than all the books that infidels ever wrote. I do not fear infidel lectures half as much as the cold and dead formalism in the professing church at the present time. One prayer meeting like the one the disciples had on the day of Pentecost would shake the whole infidel fraternity. What we want is to get hold of God in prayer.

We are not going to reach the masses by great sermons. We want to "move the arm that moves the world." To do that, we must be clean and right before God. As we read in 1 John:

> For if our heart condemn us, God is greater than our heart, and knows all things. Beloved, if our heart condemn us not, then we have confidence toward God. And whatsoever we ask, we receive of Him, because we keep His commandments, and do those things that are pleasing in His sight.
> (1 John 3:20–22)

9

PRAYER AND DEVOTION

E. M. Bounds

Once, as I rode out into the woods for my health, in 1737, having alighted from my horse in a retired place, as my manner commonly had been, to walk for divine contemplation and prayer, I had a view, that for me was extraordinary, of the glory of the Son of God. ...which continued, as near as I can judge, about an hour; which kept me the greater part of the time in a flood of tears, and weeping aloud. I felt an ardency of soul to be, what I know not otherwise how to express, emptied and annihilated; to lie in the dust, and to be full of Christ alone; to love him with a holy and pure love;...to serve and follow him; and to be perfectly sanctified and made pure, with a divine and heavenly purity.[10]   —Jonathan Edwards

Devotion has great religious significance. The root meaning of devotion is "to devote to a sacred use." Thus, devotion, in its true

---

10. Jonathan Edwards, *The Works of Jonathan Edwards, A.M.* (London: Ball, Arnold, and Co., 1840), lxxxix.

sense, has to do with religious worship. It stands intimately connected with true prayer. Devotion is the particular frame of mind found in one entirely devoted to God. It is the spirit of reverence, of awe, of godly fear. It is a state of heart that appears before God in prayer and worship. It is foreign to lightness of spirit and is opposed to levity, noise, and bluster. Devotion dwells in the realm of quietness and is still before God. It is serious, thoughtful, meditative.

Devotion belongs to the inner life and lives in the closet, but it also appears in the public services of the sanctuary. It is a part of the very spirit of true worship and of the spirit of prayer.

Devotion belongs to the devout man whose thoughts and feelings are devoted to God. Such a man has a mind given up wholly to religion and possesses a strong affection for God and an ardent love for His house. Cornelius was *"a devout man, and one that feared God with all his house, which gave much alms to the people, and prayed to God always"* (Acts 10:2). *"Devout men carried Stephen to his burial"* (Acts 8:2). *"And one Ananias, a devout man according to the law"* (Acts 22:12), was sent to Saul when he was blind, to tell him what the Lord would have him do. God can wonderfully use such men, for devout men are His chosen agents in carrying forward His plans.

Prayer promotes the spirit of devotion, while devotion is favorable to the best praying. Devotion furthers prayer and helps to drive prayer home to the object that it seeks. Prayer thrives in the atmosphere of true devotion. It is easy to pray when in the spirit of devotion. The attitude of mind and the state of heart implied in devotion make prayer effectual in reaching the throne of grace. God dwells where the spirit of devotion resides. All the graces of the Spirit are nourished and grow well in the environment created by devotion. Indeed, these graces grow nowhere else but in this environment. The absence of a devotional spirit means death to the graces born in a renewed heart. True worship finds congeniality in the atmosphere made by a spirit of devotion. While prayer is helpful to devotion, at the same time, devotion reacts on prayer and helps us to pray.

Devotion engages the heart in prayer. It is not an easy task for the lips to try to pray while the heart is absent from it. The charge that God at one time made against His ancient Israel was that they honored Him with their lips while their hearts were far from Him. (See Isaiah 29:13.)

The very essence of prayer is the spirit of devotion. Without devotion, prayer is an empty form, a vain round of words. Sadly, much of this kind of prayer prevails in the church today. This is a busy age, bustling and active, and this bustling spirit has invaded the church of God. Its religious performances are many.

The church works at religion with the order, precision, and force of real machinery. But too often it works with the heartlessness of the machine. There is much of the treadmill movement in our ceaseless round and routine of religious doings. We pray without praying. We sing without singing in the Spirit and therefore without understanding. We have music without the praise of God being in it or near it. We go to church by habit and come home all too gladly when the benediction is pronounced. We read our accustomed chapter in the Bible and feel quite relieved when the task is done. We say our prayers by rote, as a schoolboy recites his lesson, and are not sorry when the amen is uttered.

Religion has to do with everything but our hearts. It engages our hands and feet, and takes hold of our voices, and lays its hands on our money, and affects even the postures of our bodies. It does not, however, take hold of our affections, our desires, our zeal, and make us serious, desperately in earnest, and cause us to be quiet and worshipful in the presence of God. Social affinities attract us to the house of God, not the spirit of the occasion. Church membership keeps us after a fashion decent in outward conduct and with some shadow of loyalty to our baptismal vows, but our hearts are not in it. They remain cold, formal, and unimpressed amid all this outward performance, while we give ourselves over to self-congratulation, thinking that we are doing wonderfully well religiously.

Why all these sad defects in our piety? Why this modern perversion of the true nature of the religion of Jesus Christ? Why is the modern type of religion so much like a jewel case with the precious jewels gone? Why so much of this handling religion with the hands, often not too clean or unsoiled, and so little of it felt in the heart and witnessed in the life?

———

THE GREAT LACK OF MODERN RELIGION IS THE SPIRIT OF DEVOTION. WE HEAR SERMONS IN THE SAME SPIRIT WITH WHICH WE LISTEN TO A LECTURE OR HEAR A SPEECH. WE VISIT THE HOUSE OF GOD JUST AS IF IT WERE A COMMON PLACE, ON A LEVEL WITH THE THEATER, THE LECTURE HALL, OR THE FORUM.

———

The great lack of modern religion is the spirit of devotion. We hear sermons in the same spirit with which we listen to a lecture or hear a speech. We visit the house of God just as if it were a common place, on a level with the theater, the lecture hall, or the forum. We look upon the minister of God not as the divinely called man of God, but merely as a sort of public speaker, on a plane with the politician, the lawyer, or the average speech maker or lecturer. Oh, how the spirit of true and genuine devotion would radically change all this for the better! We handle sacred things just as if they were the things of the world. Even the sacrament of the Lord's Supper becomes a mere religious performance, with no preparation for it beforehand and no meditation and prayer afterward. Likewise, the sacrament of baptism has lost much of its solemnity and degenerated into a mere form with nothing special in it.

We need the spirit of devotion, not only to be salt in our secular ac-tivities, but to make our prayers real prayers. We need to put the spirit of devotion into Monday's business as well as in Sunday's worship. We need the spirit of devotion to always recollect the presence of God, to always be doing the will of God, and to always direct all things to the glory of God.

The spirit of devotion puts God in all things. It puts God not merely in our praying and churchgoing, but in all the concerns of life. *"Whether therefore you eat, or drink, or whatsoever you do, do all to the glory of God"* (1 Corinthians 10:31). The spirit of devotion makes the common things of earth sacred, and the little things great. With this spirit of devotion, we go to the workplace on Monday directed and inspired by the very same influence by which we went to church on Sunday. The spirit of devotion makes a Sabbath out of Saturday and transforms the shop or the office into a temple of God.

The spirit of devotion removes religion from being a thin veneer and puts it into the very life and being of our souls. With it, religion ceases to be merely doing a work and becomes a heart, sending its rich blood through every artery and beating with the pulsations of vigorous and radiant life.

The spirit of devotion is not merely the aroma of religion, but the stalk and stem on which religion grows. It is the salt that penetrates and makes savory all religious acts. It is the sugar that sweetens duty, self-denial, and sacrifice. It is the bright coloring that relieves the dullness of religious performances. It dispels frivolity, drives away all skin-deep forms of worship, and makes worship a serious and deep-seated service that impregnates body, soul, and spirit with its heavenly infusion. Let us ask in all seriousness: Has this highest angel of heaven, this heavenly spirit of devotion, this brightest and best angel of earth, left us? When the angel of devotion has gone, the angel of prayer has lost its wings, and it becomes a deformed and loveless thing.

The ardor of devotion is in prayer. In Revelation 4:8, we read, *"And they rest not day and night, saying, Holy, holy, holy, Lord God Almighty, which was, and is, and is to come."* The inspiration and center of their rapturous devotion is the holiness of God. That holiness of God claims their attention and inflames their devotion. There is nothing cold, nothing dull, nothing wearisome about them or their heavenly worship. *"They rest not day and night."* What zeal! What unfainting ardor and ceaseless rapture! The ministry of prayer, if it be anything worthy of the name, is a ministry of ardor, a ministry of unwearied and intense longing after God and after His holiness.

The spirit of devotion pervades the saints in heaven and characterizes the worship of heaven's angelic intelligences. No devotionless creatures are in that heavenly world. God is there, and His very presence begets the spirit of reverence, of awe, and of filial fear. If we would be partakers with them after death, we must first learn the spirit of devotion on earth before we get there.

These living creatures, in their relentless, tireless attitude toward God and their rapt devotion to His holiness, are the perfect symbols and illustrations of true prayer and its ardor. Prayer must be aflame. Its ardor must consume us. Prayer without fervor is as a sun without light or heat, or as a flower without beauty or fragrance. A soul devoted to God is a fervent soul, and prayer is the creature of that flame. Only he who is all aglow for holiness, for God, and for heaven can truly pray.

Activity is not strength. Work is not zeal. Moving about is not devotion. Activity often is the unrecognized symptom of spiritual weakness. It may be hurtful to piety when made the substitute for real devotion in worship. The colt is much more active than its mother, but she is the wheelhorse of the team, pulling the load without noise or bluster or show. The child is more active than the father, who may be bearing the rule and burdens of an empire on his heart and shoulders. Enthusiasm is more active than faith, though it cannot move mountains nor call into action any of the omnipotent forces that faith can command.

A feeble, lively, showy religious activity may spring from many causes. There is much running around, much stirring about, much going here and there, in present-day church life. However, sadly, the spirit of genuine, heartfelt devotion is strangely lacking. If there is real spiritual life, a deep-toned activity will spring from it. But it is an activity springing from strength and not from weakness. It is an activity that has deep roots, many and strong.

In the nature of things, religion must show much of its growth above ground. Much will be seen and be evident to the eye. The flower and fruit of a holy life, abounding in good works, must be seen. It cannot be otherwise. But the surface growth must be based on a vigorous growth of unseen life and hidden roots. The roots of religion must go down deep in the renewed nature to be seen on the outside. The external must have a deep internal groundwork. There must be much of the invisible and the underground growth, or else the life will be feeble and short-lived, and the external growth sickly and fruitless.

In the book of the prophet Isaiah these words are written:

They that wait upon the Lord *shall renew their strength; they shall mount up with wings as eagles; they shall run, and not be weary; and they shall walk, and not faint.*   (Isaiah 40:31)

This is the genesis of the whole matter of activity and strength of the most energetic, exhaustless, and untiring nature. All this is the result of waiting on God.

There may be much activity induced by drill or created by enthusiasm, the product of the weakness of the flesh, and the inspiration of volatile, shortlived forces. Activity continues often at the expense of more solid, useful elements and generally to the total neglect of prayer. To be too busy with God's work to commune with God, to be busy with doing church work without taking time to talk to God about His work, is the highway to backsliding. Many people have walked there to the hurt of their immortal souls. Notwithstanding great activity, great enthusiasm, and much hurrah for the work, the work and the activity will be but blindness without the cultivation and the maturity of the graces of prayer.

10

THE RESULTS OF DEFINITE
AND DETERMINED PRAYER

R. A. Torrey

The effectual fervent prayer of a righteous man availeth much.
(James 5:16 KJV)

These words of God set forth prayer as a working force, as a force that brings things to pass that would not come to pass if it were not for prayer. This truth comes out even more clearly in the American Standard Version: "*The supplication of a righteous man availeth much in its working.*" While this translation means practically the same thing as the King James Version, it is not only a more accurate translation, but it is also a more suggestive one. It tells us that prayer is something that works, and that it avails much because of its "*working.*" Yes, prayer certainly does work.

A contrast is often drawn by many between praying and working. I knew a man once, an officer in a Sunday school in Brooklyn. One day the superintendent called on him to pray. He arose and said, "I am not a praying Christian; I am a working Christian." But praying is working. It is the most effective work that anyone can do; that is, we can often bring more to pass by praying than we can by any other form of effort we might put forth.

Furthermore, prayer, if it is real prayer, the kind of prayer that avails much with God, oftentimes is harder work than any other kind of effort; it takes more out of a person than any other kind of effort. When Mr. Charles M. Alexander and I went to Liverpool for our second series of meetings there, Rev. Musgrave Brown, vicar of one of the leading Church of England parishes in the city, was chairman of our committee. His health gave out the very first week of the meetings, and he was ordered to Switzerland by his doctor. Soon after reaching Switzerland, he wrote me saying, "I hoped to be of so much help in these meetings and anticipated so much from them, but here I am, way off here in Switzerland, ordered here by my doctor, and now all I can do is to pray." Then he added, "But after all, that is the greatest thing anyone can do, is it not? And real prayer takes more out of a person than anything else, does it not?" Yes, it often does. Real praying is a costly exercise, but it pays far more than it costs. It is not easy work, but it is the most profitable of all work. We can accomplish more by time and strength put into prayer than we can by putting the same amount of time and strength into anything else.

You will notice that in the American Standard Version the word *"supplication"* is substituted for the word *"prayer."* The reason for this is that there are a number of Greek words that are translated *"prayer"* in the King James Version, and they have different shades of meaning, sometimes very significant shades of meaning. The Greek word that the King James Version translates *"prayer"* in this passage is a very significant word: it sets forth prayer as the definite expression of a deeply felt need. Indeed, the primary meaning of the word is "need." Therefore, our text teaches that definite and determined prayer to God *"availeth much."*

The Greek word translated *"availeth"* is also an expressive and significant word. Its primary meaning is "to be strong," "to have power or force," and then "to exercise power." So the thought of our text is that definite and determined prayer exerts much power in its working, that it achieves great things. Then in the verses that immediately follow our text, we are told of the astounding things Elijah brought to pass by his prayers, how he shut up heaven for three years and six months so that there was not a drop of rain for that long period. The Old Testament account tells us that not only was there not a drop of rain, but furthermore, not a drop of dew. (See 1 Kings 17:1.) When the proper time had come, Elijah *prayed again, and the heaven gave rain, and the earth brought forth her fruit* (James 5:18 KJV). Or as Mr. D. L. Moody used to put it in his graphic way, "Elijah locked up heaven for three years and six months and put the key in his pocket."

Now there is no particular reason that you or I know of why we should shut up heaven for three years and six months, or, for that matter, for three days; but there is a most imperative need that we bring some other things to pass. There is no other way in which we can bring them to pass than by praying for them, by definite and determined prayer. So we are brought face-to-face with the tremendously important question: what are some of the definite things that are greatly to be desired at the present time that prayer will bring to pass?

We have already seen two immeasurably important things that prayer will accomplish: first, it will promote our own personal piety, our individual holiness, our individual growth into the likeness of our Lord and Savior Jesus Christ; second, it will bring the power of God into our work. Now we will discover from a study of the Bible some other exceedingly important things that the right sort of praying will bring to pass.

PRAYER WILL SAVE OTHERS

Turn to 1 John 5:16, where we read, *"If any man see his brother sin a sin which is not to death, he shall ask, and He shall give him life for them that sin not to death."*

This is one of the most remarkable statements in the whole Bible on the subject of prayer and its amazing power. The statement of this verse is not only most remarkable, but it is also most cheering and most gladdening. Here God tells us that prayer will not only bring blessing to the one who prays, but that it will also bring the greatest of all blessings to others, even the blessing of eternal life to those for whom we pray. It tells us that if we see another sinning a sin not unto death—that is, committing sin, any sin except the one unpardonable sin—we can go to God in prayer for that person, and in answer to our prayers, God will give eternal life to this one for whom we have prayed.

This passage, of course, is often taken to teach divine healing and is interpreted as if the thought were that the *"life"* here spoken of was mere natural or physical life. People take this verse to mean that by our prayer, we can get physical life for one who is sick because of his sinning, but who has not committed the sin that would bring about his being removed from this world. But this interpretation is not only incorrect but also impossible. The apostle John in his writings used two different Greek words for "life." One signifies physical life, and the other signifies spiritual or eternal life. I have looked up every passage where John used this latter word in his gospel, in his epistles, and in the book of Revelation, and in not one single instance did he use the word used in this verse for anything but spiritual or eternal life. This is the word John used in this passage, and the thought of this passage then is, not that one may obtain physical life, deliverance from natural death, by praying for one who has sinned, but that he can obtain eternal life, salvation in its fullest sense, for the one who has sinned but has not sinned unto death. This is a wonderful thought and a thought full of comfort and encouragement.

WE CAN ACCOMPLISH MORE FOR THE
SALVATION OF OTHERS BY PRAYING FOR THEM
THAN WE CAN IN ANY OTHER WAY.

We can accomplish more for the salvation of others by praying for them than we can in any other way. I do not mean by this that when we feel our responsibility for the salvation of someone else, we should merely pray for them and do nothing else. That is what many do; they are not willing to do their duty and go to them and speak to them about Christ, and so they go to God in prayer. Then, when they have prayed for their salvation, they flatter themselves that they have done their whole duty, and thus make their prayer an excuse for their cowardice and laziness and neglect of duty. That kind of praying is a mockery. It is simply an attempt to cover up and excuse our neglect of duty, and God will pay no attention whatsoever to prayers of that sort. God never gave us the wonderful privilege of prayer as a makeshift to cover up our laziness and neglect of duty. But if we are willing that God should use us in answering our own prayers, willing to do anything that God may guide us to do in order to secure the salvation of those for whom we are praying, willing to do anything in our power to bring about the salvation of those for whom we pray, then we can accomplish far more for their salvation by praying for them than in any other way.

Did you ever think how our Lord Jesus Himself accomplished things by praying that even He could not accomplish in any other way? Take for example the case of Simon Peter. He was full of self-confidence and therefore was in imminent danger. Our Lord endeavored by His teachings and by His warnings to deliver Peter from his self-confidence. He told Peter definitely of his coming temptation and of his fall, but Peter, filled with self-confidence, replied, *"Though all men shall be offended because of You, yet will I never be offended"* (Matthew 26:33), and again, *"I will lay down my life for Your sake"* (John 13:37). Teaching failed, warning failed, and then our Lord took to prayer. He said,

> *Simon, Simon, behold, Satan has desired to have you, that he may sift you as wheat: but I have prayed for you, that your faith fail not: and when you are converted, strengthen your brethren.*
>
> (Luke 22:31–32)

Satan got what he asked—he had Simon in his sieve and sifted him; and, oh, how poor Simon was battered and bruised against the edges of Satan's sieve! But all the time Satan sifted, our Lord Jesus prayed, and Simon was perfectly safe even though he was in Satan's sieve. All that Satan succeeded in doing with him was to sift some of the chaff out of him, and Simon came out of Satan's sieve purer than he ever was before.

It was our Lord's prayer for him that transformed the Simon who denied his Lord three times, and denied Him with oaths and curses, in the courtyard of Annas and Caiaphas, into Peter, the man of rock. This transformed Peter faced the very court that sentenced Jesus to death and hurled defiance in their teeth and said,

> *Rulers of the people, and elders of Israel, if we this day be examined of the good deed done to the impotent man, by what means he is made whole; be it known to you all, and to all the people of Israel, that by the name of Jesus Christ of Nazareth, whom you crucified, whom God raised from the dead, even by Him does this man stand here before you whole.* (Acts 4:8–10)

Prayer will reach down, down, down into the deepest depths of sin and ruin and take hold of men and women who seem lost beyond all possibility or hope of redemption, and lift them up, up, up until they are fit for a place beside the Son of God upon the throne.

Many years ago in Chicago, in the early days of D. L. Moody's work in that city, there was a desperate man who used to attend the meetings and try to disturb them. He was a Scotchman and had been reared in a Christian home by a godly mother, but he had wandered far from the teachings of his childhood. This man was dreaded even by other dissolute men in Chicago. One night he stood outside the old Tabernacle with a pitcher of beer in his hand offering a free drink to everyone who came out of the Tabernacle. At other times, he would come into the meetings and into the after-meetings and try to disturb the workers.

One night Major D. W. Whittle was dealing with two young men, and this desperate Scotchman stood nearby mocking, until Major

Whittle turned to the young men and said, "If you set any value upon your souls, I advise you not to have anything to do with that desperate man." The Scotchman only laughed, but his old mother over in Scotland was praying. One night he went to bed just as wicked and godless as ever, and in answer to his mother's prayer, God awakened him in the middle of the night and brought to his mind a text of Scripture that he had forgotten was in the Bible, Romans 4:5: *"But to him that works not, but believes on Him that justifies the ungodly, his faith is counted for righteousness."* That verse of Scripture went home to his heart, and he accepted Christ without getting out of bed. He became one of the most active and most useful members of the Moody Church. When I was pastor of the church, he was one of the elders, and he afterward became visitor for the church and was used by God to lead many to Christ.

Sometime after his own conversion, he went to Scotland to visit his old mother. He had a brother in Glasgow in business, and this brother was trying to be an agnostic. But the godly mother and converted son prayed for this brother, and he was converted and gave himself up to God's work. This brother went to the Free Church College to prepare for foreign missionary work, and for thirty years he was a medical missionary in India under the Free Church of Scotland Missionary Board. But there was still another brother, a wanderer on the face of the earth. They did not know where he was, though they supposed he was somewhere on the high seas, but the godly mother and converted brother knelt and prayed for this wandering son and brother. As they prayed, that son, unknown to them, was on the deck of a vessel on the other side of the globe, in the Bay of Bengal, not far from Calcutta. The Spirit of God fell upon that son on the deck of that vessel, and he was converted. He was for many years a member of the Moody Church when I was pastor there. When I went out to Los Angeles he followed me and became a member of our church in Los Angeles, and then died a triumphant death. Prayer had reached halfway around the world and instantly saved a man who seemed utterly beyond hope.

When I was in England holding meetings in the city of Manchester, one of the leading businessmen came to me and asked me to pray for the conversion of his son. He said, "My son is a graduate of Cambridge University and a brilliant lawyer. He has a wife and two children but he has left them, and we do not know where he is. Will you pray for his conversion?" I promised him that I would. Some months afterward, this man came to me at the Keswick Convention and said, "I have found my boy. He is in Vancouver, British Columbia. Do you know any minister in Vancouver to whom I could cable?" I told him the name of a friend who was a minister of the gospel in Vancouver, and he cabled him. The next day, he came to me and said, "We were too late; the bird has flown; he has left Vancouver. Will you continue to pray for him?" I said I would. At the close of the same year, when we began our second series of meetings in Liverpool, unknown to his father, this son had returned to England and was in Liverpool. He came to our first Sunday afternoon meeting and was one of the first ones to accept Christ. Immediately he began to study for holy orders under the bishop of Liverpool.

Do you have loved ones who are unsaved? There is a way to reach them: that way is by the throne of God. By the way of the throne of God, you can reach out to the uttermost parts of the earth and get hold of your loved ones of whom you have lost track. God knows where they are, and God hears and answers prayer. At the close of the meeting in a certain city, a lady came to me and said, "I have a brother above sixty years of age. I have been praying for his salvation for years, but I have given up. I will begin again." Within two weeks she came to me and said, "I have heard from my brother, and he has accepted Christ."

Yes, yes, yes, *"the supplication of a righteous man availeth much in its working,"* and if we would only pray more and be more sure that we had met the conditions of prevailing prayer, we would see multitudes more of men and women flocking to Jesus Christ. Oh, that we might pray as we ought, as intelligently as we ought, as definitely as we ought, as earnestly and determinedly as we ought, for the salvation of the men, women, and children whom we know are unsaved!

PRAYER BRINGS BLESSING AND POWER

And take the helmet of salvation, and the sword of the Spirit, which is the word of God: praying always with all prayer and supplication in the Spirit, and watching thereto with all perseverance and supplication for all saints; and for me, that utterance may be given to me, that I may open my mouth boldly, to make known the mystery of the gospel, for which I am an ambassador in bonds: that therein I may speak boldly, as I ought to speak. (Ephesians 6:17–20)

Here Paul urgently requested the earnest prayers of the believers in Ephesus for himself, that in answer to their prayers he might preach the gospel with boldness and with power. Paul made a similar request of every church to which he wrote with one striking exception; that one exception was the church in Galatia. That church was a backsliding church, and he did not care to have a backsliding church praying for him. In every other case, he urged the church to pray for him. Here we see the power of prayer to bring blessing and boldness and effectiveness to ministers of the gospel. A minister may be made a man of power by prayer, and he may be bereft of power by people failing to pray for him. Any church may have a mighty man of God for its pastor, if it is willing to pay the price, and that price is not a big salary but great praying.

A MINISTER MAY BE MADE A MAN OF POWER BY PRAYER, AND HE MAY BE BEREFT OF POWER BY PEOPLE FAILING TO PRAY FOR HIM. ANY CHURCH MAY HAVE A MIGHTY MAN OF GOD FOR ITS PASTOR, IF IT IS WILLING TO PAY THE PRICE, AND THAT PRICE IS NOT A BIG SALARY BUT GREAT PRAYING.

Do you have a pastor you do not like, a pastor who is perhaps inefficient, or does not clearly know or preach the truth? Do you want a new minister? I can tell you how to get him. Pray for the one you have until God makes him over.

Many years ago in one of the Cornish parishes of the Church of England, the vicar was not even a converted man. He had little interest in the real things of God; his interest was largely in restoring old churches and in matters of ritual. There were many godly people in that parish, and they began to pray to God to convert their minister, and then they would go to church every Sunday and watch for the answer to their prayers. One Sunday when he rose to speak, he had not uttered many sentences before the people of spiritual discernment realized that their prayers had been answered and a cry arose all over the church, "The parson's converted, the parson's converted!" And it was true. He was not only converted, but he was filled with *"power from on high"* (Luke 24:49). For many years afterward, God used that man all over England for the conversion of sinners, for the blessing of all saints, and for the quickening of churches, as almost no other man in the Church of England.

There was a church in the city of Hartford, Connecticut, that had a very brilliant man for its pastor. But the pastor was not sound in doctrine. There were three godly men in that church who realized that their pastor was not preaching the truth. However, they did not go around the congregation stirring up dissatisfaction with the pastor. They covenanted together to meet every Saturday night to pray long into the night for their minister. So Saturday night after Saturday night they met in earnest and extended prayer; then Sunday morning, they would go to church and sit in their places and watch for an answer to their prayers. One Sunday morning when the minister rose to speak, he was just as brilliant and just as gifted as ever, but it soon became evident that God had transformed his ideas and transformed the man. Through that minister who was transformed by the prayers of his members, God sent to the city of Hartford the greatest revival that city ever had. Oh, if we would talk less to one another against our ministers, and more to God on their behalf, we would have far better ministers than we have now.

Do you have a minister whom you do like? Do you wish him to be even better; do you wish him to be far more effective than he is today? Pray for him until God gives him new wisdom and clothes him with new power.

Have you ever heard how D. L. Moody became a worldwide evangelist? After the great fire in Chicago, Mr. Moody stayed in Chicago long enough to get money together to feed the poor and to provide a new building for his own work, and then he went to England for a rest. He did not intend to preach at all, but to hear some of the great preachers on the other side of the water—Charles Spurgeon, George Müller, and others. He was invited to preach one Sunday in a Congregational church in the north part of London, of which a Mr. John Lessey was the pastor. He accepted the invitation. Sunday morning, as he preached, he had great difficulty. As he told the story to me many years afterward, he said,

I had no power, no liberty; it seemed like pulling a heavy train up a steep grade, and as I preached I said to myself, "What a fool I was to consent to preach. I came here to hear others, and here I am preaching." As I drew to the close of my sermon, I had a sense of relief that I was so near through, and then the thought came to me, "Well, I've got to do it again tonight." I tried to get Mr. Lessey to release me from preaching that night, but he would not consent. I went to the evening service with a heavy heart. But I had not been preaching long when it seemed as if the powers of an unseen world had fallen upon that audience. As I drew to the close of my sermon, I got courage to draw the net. I asked all who would then and there accept Christ to rise, and about five hundred people rose to their feet. I thought there must be some mistake; so I asked them to sit down, and then I said, "There will be an after-meeting in the vestry, and if any of you will really accept Christ, meet the pastor and me in the vestry."

There was a door at each side of the pulpit into the vestry, and people began to stream through these doors into the vestry. I turned to Mr. Lessey and said, "Mr. Lessey, who are these people?" He replied, "I do not know." "Are they your people?" "Some of them are." "Are they Christians?" "Not as far as I know." We went into the vestry, and I repeated the invitation in a stronger form, and they all rose again. I still thought that there must be some mistake and asked them to be seated, and repeated the invitation in a still stronger form, and again they all rose. I still thought there must be some mistake and I said to the people, "I am going to Ireland tomorrow, but your pastor will be here tomorrow night if you really mean what you have said here tonight meet him here." After I reached Ireland, I received a telegram from Mr. Lessey, saying, "Mr. Moody, there were more people out on Monday night than on Sunday night. A revival has broken out in our church, and you must come back and help me."

Mr. Moody hurried back from Dublin to London and held a series of meetings in Mr. Lessey's church that added hundreds of people to the churches of North London. That was what led to the invitation that took him over to England later for the great work that stirred the whole world.

After Mr. Moody had told me that story, I said, "Mr. Moody, someone must have been praying." He said,

Oh, did I not tell you that? That is the point of the whole story. There were two sisters in that church, one of whom was bedridden; the other one heard me that Sunday morning. She went home and said to her sister, "Who do you suppose preached for us this morning?" The sister replied, "I do not know." Then she said, "Guess," and the sister guessed all the men that Mr. Lessey was in the habit of exchanging with, but her sister said it was none of them. Then her sister asked, "Who did preach for us this morning?" And she replied, "Mr. Moody of Chicago." No sooner had she said it than her sister turned pale as death and said, "What! Mr. Moody of Chicago! I have read of him in an American paper, and I have been praying God to send him to London, to our church. If I had known he was to preach this morning, I would have eaten no breakfast; I would have spent the whole morning in fasting and prayer. Now, sister, go out, lock the door, do not let any one come to see me, do not let them send me any dinner; I am going to spend the whole afternoon and evening in fasting and prayer!" And pray she did, and God heard and answered.

God is just as ready to hear and answer you as He was to answer that bedridden saint. To whatever church you belong, and whoever your pastor is, you can make him a man of power. If he is a man of power already, you can make him a man of even greater power.

Will you bear with me while I give you a page out of my own experience? When I went to Chicago, it was not to take the pastorate of a church but to be superintendent of the Bible Institute and of the Chicago Evangelization Society. After I had been there four years, the pulpit of the Moody Church became vacant, and Mr. Moody and I asked them to call a very gifted preacher from Aberdeen, Scotland, which they did. While we waited to hear from him as to whether he would accept the call, I filled the pulpit; and God so blessed the preaching of His Word that quite a number of the people were praying that the minister from Scotland would not accept the call, and he did not. Then they called me to the pastorate. I could not see how I could take it; my hands were full with the Institute, the lectures, the correspondence, and other duties. But Mr. Moody urged me to accept the call; he said, "That is what I have been wanting all the time. If you will only accept the call, I will give you all the help that you ask for, and provide men to help you in the Institute." And so I accepted the call.

The first sermon I preached after taking the pastorate of the church was upon prayer, and in it I said some of the things that I have said here. As I drew toward the close of my sermon I said, "How glad your new pastor would be if he knew that some of you men and women of God sat up late Saturday night, or rose early Sunday morning, to pray for your new pastor." Many of those dear saints of God took me at my word. Many of them sat up late Saturday night praying for their minister, and many of them rose early Sunday morning to pray for their minister, and God answered their prayers.

When I took the pastorate, the church building would seat 2,200 people—1,200 on the first floor and 1,000 in the gallery. But in the preceding years, only the first floor of the church had been filled, and the gallery only opened on special occasions, when Mr. Moody was there or something of that kind. Almost immediately upon my being instated, it became necessary to open the gallery. Then in the evening service, every inch of standing room would be taken, until we packed 2,700 people into that building by actual count, and the police authorities allowed us no longer to let people sit on the stairs or stand in the aisles. Then we had an overflow meeting in the rooms below, which would seat 1,100, and oftentimes into the Institute Lecture Hall also.

But that was not the best of it. There were conversions every Sunday; indeed, there were conversions in and around the church practically every day in the week. The great majority of those who were converted did not unite with the Moody Church; they were strangers passing through the city, or people who came from other churches. It came to be quite a custom for some ministers to send their people over to our church to have them converted, then they would go back and join the churches to which they properly belonged. So only a comparatively small proportion of those converted united with our church, and yet the smallest number that we ever received into the church in any one of the eight years I remained there as active pastor was 250. And in those eight years I had the joy of giving the right hand of fellowship to over 2,000 new members.

And it went on just the same way the four years that I was only nominally pastor and not at the church at all, under the different men who came and whom the people prayed into power. It went on the same way under Dr. A. C. Dixon's pastorate. It was not so much the men who were preaching as the people behind them who were praying that accomplished such great things for God. Then when I started around the world, those people still followed me with their prayers; and it was reported when I came back, by one who claimed to know, that there were more than 102,000 people who made a definite profession of accepting Christ in the different places I visited in those months that I was away. When I came back after my first eighteen months' absence, Dr. Dixon met me one day, and he said to me (this was before he became pastor of the church), "Brother Torrey, when we heard the things that were done in Australia and elsewhere, we were all surprised. We didn't think it was in you." He was perfectly right about that; it wasn't in me. Then he added, "But when I went out and supplied your church for a month and heard your people pray for you, I understood." Oh, any church can have a minister who is a man of power, a minister who is baptized and filled with the Holy Spirit, if they are willing to pay the price, and the price is prayer, much prayer, and much real prayer, prayer in the Holy Spirit.

11

PREVAILING PRAYER

Charles Finney

The effectual, fervent prayer of a righteous man avails much.
(James 5:16)

There are two goals necessary for a revival: one is to influence men, and the other is to influence God. The truth is employed to influence men, and prayer is employed to move God. When I speak of moving God, I do not mean that God's mind is changed by prayer or that His disposition or character is changed. Prayer produces such a change in us that God is completely consistent with His nature when He answers our prayers.

When a sinner repents, his state of feeling makes it proper for God to forgive him. God has always been ready to forgive men on that condition. Therefore, when the sinner changes his feelings and repents, it requires no change of feeling in God to pardon him. It is the sinner's repentance that renders His forgiveness proper. This is when God will act.

Some people don't make the mistake of overemphasizing the role of prayer in "changing" God's mind, but they overlook the fact that prayer could be offered forever, by itself, apart from the work of the Holy Spirit, and nothing would be accomplished.

SPECIFIC PRAYERS

Many people go to their rooms alone "to pray," simply because "they must say their prayers." The time of day has come when they are in the habit of praying—in the morning, at noon, or at whatever time of day it may be. But instead of having anything to say, any definite reason on their minds, they fall down on their knees and simply pray for whatever floats into their imaginations. When they have finished, they can hardly remember what they have been praying for. This is not effective prayer.

To pray effectively, you must pray with submission to the will of God. Do not confuse submission with indifference. No two things are more unlike. I once knew an individual who came to a revival. He was cold and did not enter into the spirit of prayer. When he heard believers praying as if they could not be denied, he was shocked at their boldness. He insisted on the importance of praying with submission. Yet it was plain that he confused submission with indifference.

CRUCIAL PRAYER

If the will of God is not known, submission without prayer is tempting God. For all you know, your prayer may be the thing on which an event turns. In the case of an impenitent friend, your prayers may be the key to his being saved.

Christians often amaze themselves when they look back on their ardent, bold prayers spoken in a moment of intense emotion. Yet these prayers have prevailed and obtained the blessing. And many of these people are among the holiest people I know in the world.

EFFECTIVE MOTIVES

The temptation to have selfish motives is so strong that there is reason to fear that a great many parental prayers never rise above the yearnings of parental tenderness. That is why so many prayers are not answered and why so many pious, praying parents have ungodly children. Prayer for the unsaved must be based on more than sympathy. Missionaries and others often make the mistake of praying only about those going to hell, forgetting prayer about how the unsaved also dishonor God.

Most Christians work up to prevailing prayer through a prolonged process. Their minds gradually become filled with anxiety about something, until they even go about their business sighing out their desires to God. It is like the mother whose child is sick who constantly sighs as if her heart would break. If she is a praying mother, her sighs are breathed out to God all day long. If she leaves the room where her child is, her mind is still on her baby. If she is asleep, her thoughts are still on her child. She will even jerk in her dreams, thinking that perhaps her child may be dying. Her whole mind is absorbed with that sick child. This is the state of mind in which Christians offer prevailing prayer.

THE DEPTH OF CONCERN

The spirit of those who have been in distress for the souls of others is similar to that of the apostle Paul, who worked for souls and was ready to wish himself cut off from Christ for the sake of others. (See Romans 9:1–3.)

The psalmist showed the same concern when he prayed, *"Horror has taken hold upon me because of the wicked that forsake Your law.... Rivers of water run down my eyes, because they keep not Your law"* (Psalm 119:53, 136). The prophet Jeremiah also experienced great sorrow because of Israel's sins: *"I am pained at my very heart; my heart makes a noise in me; I cannot hold my peace, because you have heard, O my soul, the sound of the trumpet, the alarm of war"* (Jeremiah 4:19). In view of this, why should people be considered crazy if they cannot help but cry out loud when they think of the misery of those who are going to eternal destruction?

If you plan to pray effectively, you must pray a lot. It was said of the apostle James that, after his death, people noticed his knees were calloused, like a camel's, from praying so much. Ah, here was the secret of the success of those first ministers! They had calloused knees!

USING THE NAME

If you intend to pray effectively, you must offer your prayers in the name of Christ. You cannot come to God in your own name. You cannot plead your own merits. But you can come in a name that is always acceptable. You know what it is to use the name of a man. If you were to go to the bank with a check endorsed by a millionaire (which would be the equivalent of his giving you his name), you know you could get the money from the bank as easily as he could. In the same way, Jesus Christ gives you the use of His name. When you pray in the name of Christ, you can prevail just as well as He and receive just as much as God's beloved Son would if He were to pray for the same things. You must pray in faith.

These strong desires behind the prevailing prayer I mentioned are the natural results of great benevolence and a clear view of the danger for sinners. This is a reasonable sentiment. If the average Christian were to see a home burning, hear the shrieks of the family inside, and see their agony, he or she would be extremely upset—perhaps even sick. No one would consider these reactions strange. In fact, if they had no powerful reaction, they would be considered coldhearted.

THE NECESSITY OF A LOVING CHARACTER

Why is it, then, that Christians are thought of as lunatics for their concern about the awful danger sinners are in? The fact is, those individuals who have never felt such concern have never felt real benevolence and must have a very superficial Christian love. I do not mean to judge harshly or speak unkindly, but it is a simple fact that a person without such a loving character is a superficial believer. This is not being critical; it is the plain truth.

When Christians are driven to the extreme, they make a desperate effort and roll the burden on the Lord Jesus Christ. They exercise a childlike confidence in Him. Then they feel relieved, as if assured that the soul they were praying for will be saved. The burden is gone, and God seems to kindly soothe the mind with a sweet assurance that the blessing will be granted.

Often, after a Christian has had this struggle, this agony in prayer, and has obtained relief in this way, he finds that the sweetest and most heavenly affections flow out. His soul rests sweetly and gloriously in God and rejoices *"with joy unspeakable and full of glory"* (1 Peter 1:8).

BINDING PRAYER

This travailing in prayer for souls also creates a remarkable bond between warmhearted Christians and young converts. Those who are converted are very dear to those who have had this spirit of prayer for them. The feeling is like that of a mother for her firstborn child. Paul expressed it beautifully when he said, *"My little children, of whom I travail in birth again until Christ be formed in you"* (Galatians 4:19). They had backslidden, and he suffered all the agonies of a parent over a wandering child. In revival, I have often noticed how those who had the spirit of prayer loved the young converts. To those who have never felt this love, what I have described does not make sense.

PROTECTING PRAYER

Another reason God requires this sort of prayer is that it is the only way in which the church can be properly prepared to receive great blessings without being injured by them. When the church is thus prostrated in the dust before God, and is in the depths of agony in prayer, the blessing does it good. However, if the church receives the blessing without this deep humility of soul, it grows puffed up with pride. But if it is in the proper attitude, it increases in holiness, love, and humility.

INTENSE, PREVAILING PRAYER

A minister once related a story to me about a town that had not had a revival in many years. The church was nearly extinct, the youth were all unconverted, and desolation reigned unbroken. There lived, in a secluded part of the town, an aged blacksmith who stammered so badly that it was painful to hear him speak. One Friday, as he worked in his shop, alone, he became very upset about the state of the church and of the impenitent. His agony became so great that he had to put away his work, lock the shop door, and spend the afternoon in prayer.

He continued to pray all day. Then he asked his minister to arrange a conference meeting. After some hesitation, the minister consented, even though he feared few people would attend. He called the meeting for the same evening at a large private house. When evening came, more people assembled than could be accommodated in the house. All were silent for a time, until one sinner broke out in tears and said, "If anyone can pray, will he pray for me?" Another followed, and another, and still another, until people from every part of town were under deep conviction. It was also remarkable that they all dated their conviction to the hour the old man prayed in his shop. A powerful revival followed. Thus, this stammering old man's prayers prevailed, and as a prince, he had power with God. (See Genesis 32:28.)

12

THE EXAMPLE OF OUR LORD

Andrew Murray

The connection between the prayer life and the Spirit life is close and indissoluble. It is not merely that we can receive the Spirit through prayer, but the Spirit life requires, as an indispensable thing, a continuous prayer life. I can be led continually by the Spirit only as I continually give myself to prayer.

This was very evident in the life of our Lord. A study of His life will give us a wonderful view of the power and holiness of prayer.

Consider His baptism. It was when He was baptized and prayed that heaven was opened and the Holy Spirit came down upon Him. (See Luke 3:21–22.) God desired to crown Christ's surrender of Himself to the sinner's baptism in Jordan, which was also a surrender of Himself to the sinner's death, with the gift of the Spirit for the work that He must accomplish. But this could not have taken place had He not prayed. In the fellowship of worship, the Spirit was bestowed on Him to lead Him out into the desert to spend forty days in prayer and fasting. Turn to the first chapter of Mark:

And at evening, when the sun did set, they brought to Him all that were diseased, and them that were possessed with devils. And all the city was gathered together at the door.... And in the morning, rising up a great while before day, He went out, and departed into a solitary place, and there prayed.　　　(Mark 1:32–33, 35)

The work of the day and evening had exhausted Him. In His healing of the sick and casting out devils, power had gone out of Him. While others still slept, He went away to pray and to renew His strength in communion with His Father. He had need of this; otherwise He would not have been ready for the new day. The holy work of delivering souls demands constant renewal through fellowship with God.

Think again of the calling of the apostles as given in Luke:

And it came to pass in those days, that He went out into a mountain to pray, and continued all night in prayer to God. And when it was day, He called to Him His disciples: and of them He chose twelve, whom also He named apostles.　　　(Luke 6:12–13)

Is it not clear that if anyone wishes to do God's work, he must take time for fellowship with Him, to receive His wisdom and power? The dependence and helplessness of which this is an evidence open the way and give God the opportunity of revealing His power. How great was the importance of the choosing of the apostles for Christ's own work, for the early church, and for all time! It had God's blessing and seal; the stamp of prayer was on it.

Turn to Luke's gospel:

And it came to pass, as He was alone praying, His disciples were with Him: and He asked them, saying, Whom say the people that I am?... Peter answering said, The Christ of God.　　　(Luke 9:18, 20)

The Lord had intended that the Father might reveal to them who He was, and for this purpose He had chosen the twelve apostles. (See

John 17:6–8.) After a night of prayer, *"He chose twelve, whom also He named apostles"* (Luke 6:13). It was one of these, Peter, who said, *"You are the Christ, the Son of the living God"* (Matthew 16:16); and the Lord then said, *"Flesh and blood has not revealed it to you, but My Father which is in heaven"* (verse 17). This great confession was the fruit of prayer.

Read further:

> *He took Peter and John and James, and went up into a mountain to pray. And as He prayed, the fashion of His countenance was altered…. And there came a voice out of the cloud, saying, This is My beloved Son: hear Him.* (Luke 9:28–29, 35)

Christ had desired that, for the strengthening of their faith, God might give them an assurance from heaven that He was the Son of God. Prayer obtained for our Lord Jesus Himself, as well as for His disciples, what happened on the Mount of Transfiguration.

Does it not become still clearer that what God wills to accomplish on earth needs prayer as its indispensable condition? And there is but one way for Christ and believers. A heart and mouth open toward heaven in believing prayer will certainly not be put to shame.

Read Luke 11:1:

> *As He was praying in a certain place, when He ceased, one of His disciples said to Him, Lord, teach us to pray.*

And then He gave them that inexhaustible prayer: *"Our Father which are in heaven"* (verse 2). In this He showed what was going on in His heart, when He prayed that God's name might be hallowed, and His kingdom come, and His will be done, and all of this *"as in heaven, so in earth"* (verse 2). How will this ever come to pass? Through prayer. This prayer has been uttered through the ages by countless millions, to their unspeakable comfort. But do not forget this—it was born out of the prayer of our Lord Jesus. He had been praying, and therefore was able to give that glorious answer.

Read John 14:16: "*I will pray the Father, and He shall give you another Comforter.*" The entire dispensation of the New Testament, with the wonderful outpouring of the Holy Spirit, is the outcome of the prayer of the Lord Jesus. In answer to the prayer of the Lord Jesus, and later of His disciples, the Holy Spirit will surely come. But it will be in answer to prayer like that of our Lord, in which He took time to be alone with God and in that prayer offered Himself wholly to God.

Read John 17, the most holy high priestly prayer! Here the Son prays first for Himself, that the Father will glorify Him by giving Him power for the cross, by raising Him from the dead, by setting Him at His right hand. These great things could not take place except through prayer. Prayer had the power to obtain them.

Afterward, He prayed for His disciples, that the Father might preserve them from the evil one, might keep them from the world, and might sanctify them. And then, further, He prayed for all those who through their word might believe on Him, that all might be one in love, even as the Father and the Son were one.

This prayer gives us a glimpse into the wonderful relationship between the Father and the Son and teaches us that all the blessings of heaven come continually through the prayer of Him who is at God's right hand and ever prays for us. But it teaches us, also, that all these blessings must in the same manner be desired and asked for by us. The whole nature and glory of God's blessings consist in this: they must be obtained in answer to prayer, by hearts entirely surrendered to Him, and hearts that believe in the power of prayer.

Now we come to the most remarkable instance of all. In Gethsemane we see that our Lord, according to His constant habit, consulted and arranged with the Father the work He had to do on earth. First He besought Him in agony and bloody sweat to let the cup pass from Him. When He understood that this could not be, then He prayed for strength to drink it, and surrendered Himself with the words: "*Your will be done*" (Matthew 26:42). He was able to meet the enemy full of courage, and in the power of God He gave Himself over to the death of the cross. He had prayed.

Oh, why is it that God's children have so little faith in the glory of prayer as the great power for subjecting our own wills to that of God, as well as for the confident carrying out of the work of God in spite of our great weakness? If only we might learn from our Lord Jesus how impossible it is to walk with God, to obtain God's blessing or leading, or to do His work joyously and fruitfully, apart from close, unbroken fellowship with Him who is ever a living fountain of spiritual life and power!

Let every Christian think over this simple study of the prayer life of our Lord Jesus and endeavor from God's Word to learn what the life is that the Lord Jesus Christ bestows upon him and supports in him. It is nothing else than a life of daily prayer. Let each minister especially recognize how entirely vain it is to attempt to do the work of our Lord in any other way than that in which He did it. Let us, as workers, begin to believe that we are set free from the ordinary business of the world that we may, above everything, have time, in our Savior's name and with His Spirit and in oneness with Him, to ask for and obtain blessing for the world.

13

PRAYER THAT MOTIVATES GOD

E. M. Bounds

Two thirds of the praying we do is for that which would give us the greatest possible pleasure sure to receive. It is a sort of spiritual self-indulgence in which we engage and, as a consequence, is the exact opposite of self-discipline. God knows all this and keeps His children asking. In the process of time—His time—our petitions take on another aspect, and we, another spiritual approach. God keeps us praying until, in His wisdom, He is ready to answer. And no matter how long it may be before He speaks, it is, even then, far earlier than we have a right to expect or hope to deserve.   —Anonymous

The purpose of Christ's teachings is to declare that men are to pray earnestly. They are to pray with an earnestness that cannot be denied. Heaven has listening ears only for the wholehearted and the deeply earnest. Energy, courage, and perseverance must back the prayers that heaven respects and that God hears.

All these qualities of soul, so essential to effectual praying, are brought out in the parable of the man who went to his friend for bread at midnight. (See Luke 11:5–10.) This man went on his errand with confidence. Friendship promised him success. His cry was pressing. Truly, he could not go back empty-handed. The flat refusal shamed and surprised him. Here even friendship failed! But there was still something to be tried—stern resolution and fixed determination. He would stay and pursue his demand until the door was opened and the request granted. He proceeded to do this and, by persistence, secured what ordinary requesting had failed to obtain.

The success of this man, achieved in the face of a flat denial, was used by the Savior to illustrate the need for insistence in humble prayer before the throne of heavenly grace. When the answer is not immediately given, the praying Christian must gather courage at each delay. He must urgently go forward until the answer comes. The answer is assured, if he has the faith to press his petition with vigorous faith.

Negligence, faintheartedness, impatience, and fear will be fatal to our prayers. The Father's heart, hand, infinite power, and infinite willingness to hear and give to His children are waiting for the start of our insistence.

NEGLIGENCE, FAINTHEARTEDNESS, IMPATIENCE, AND FEAR WILL BE FATAL TO OUR PRAYERS. THE FATHER'S HEART, HAND, INFINITE POWER, AND INFINITE WILLINGNESS TO HEAR AND GIVE TO HIS CHILDREN ARE WAITING FOR THE START OF OUR INSISTENCE.

Persistent praying is the earnest, inward movement of the heart toward God. It is throwing the entire force of the spiritual man into the exercise of prayer. Isaiah lamented that no one stirred himself to take hold of God. There was much praying done in Isaiah's time, but it was too easy, indifferent, and complacent. There were no mighty moves by souls toward God. There was no array of sanctified energies bent on reaching and grappling with God. There was no energy to draw the treasures of His grace from Him. Forceless prayers have no power to overcome difficulties, win marked results, or gain complete victories. We must win God before we can win our plea.

Isaiah looked with hopeful eyes to the day when faith would flourish and there would be times of real praying. When those times would come, the watchmen would not weaken their vigilance, but would cry day and night. And those who were the Lord's "remembrancers" would give Him no rest. (See Isaiah 62:6–7.) Their urgent, persistent efforts would keep all spiritual interests busy and make increasing demands on God's exhaustless treasures.

Persistent praying never faints or grows weary. It is never discouraged. It never yields to cowardice but is lifted up and sustained by a hope that knows no despair and a faith that will not let go. Persistent praying has patience to wait and strength to continue. It never prepares itself to quit praying, and it refuses to get up from its knees until an answer is received.

The familiar words of the great missionary Adoniram Judson are the testimony of a man who was persistent at prayer. He said,

I was never deeply interested in any object, I never prayed sincerely and earnestly for anything but it came at some time—no matter how distant the day—somehow, in some shape, probably the last I should have devised, it came.

"Ask, and it shall be given to you; seek, and you shall find; knock, and it shall be opened to you" (Matthew 7:7). These are the ringing challenges of our Lord in regard to prayer. These challenges are His explanation that true praying must stay and advance in effort and urgency until the prayer is answered and the blessing sought is received.

In the three words *ask*, *seek*, and *knock*, Jesus, by the order in which He places them, urges the necessity of persistence in prayer. Asking, seeking, and knocking are ascending rungs in the ladder of successful prayer. No principle is more definitely enforced by Christ than that successful prayer must have in it the quality that waits and perseveres. It must have in it the courage that never surrenders, the patience that never grows tired, and the resolution that never wavers.

In the parable of the friend at midnight, a most significant and instructive lesson in this respect is outlined. Chief among the qualities included in Christ's estimate of the highest and most successful form of praying are the following: unbeatable courage, ceaseless persistence, and stability of purpose.

Persistence is made up of intensity, perseverance, and patience. The apparent delay in answering prayer is the ground and demand of persistence. In Matthew we have the first recorded instance of the miracle of healing the blind. We have an illustration of the way in which our Lord did not seem to hear immediately those who sought Him. But the two blind men continued their crying and followed Him with their continual petition saying, *"Son of David, have mercy on us"* (Matthew 9:27). But He did not answer them and went into the house. The needy ones followed Him and, finally, gained their eyesight and their plea.

The case of blind Bartimaeus is a notable one in many ways. (See Mark 10:46–52.) It is especially remarkable for the show of persistence that this blind man exhibited in appealing to our Lord. His first crying, as it seems, was done as Jesus entered Jericho, and he continued it until Jesus came out of the place. It is a strong illustration of the necessity of persistent prayer. It is also an illustration of the success that comes to those who stake their all on Christ and do not give Him any peace until He grants them their hearts' desire.

Mark put the entire incident clearly before us. At first, Jesus seems not to hear. The crowd rebukes the noisy babbling of Bartimaeus. Despite the apparent unconcern of our Lord and the rebuke of an impatient, quick-tempered crowd, the blind beggar still cries. He increases the loudness of his cry until Jesus is impressed and moved. Finally, the crowd, as well as Jesus, listens to the beggar's cry and speaks in favor of his cause. He wins his case. His persistence wins even in the face of apparent neglect on the part of Jesus and despite opposition and rebuke from the surrounding crowd. His persistence won where halfhearted indifference would surely have failed.

Faith functions in connection with prayer and, of course, has its inseparable association with persistence. But the latter quality *drives* the prayer to the believing point. A persistent spirit brings a man to the place where faith takes hold, claims, and appropriates the blessing.

The absolute necessity of persistent prayer is plainly stated in the Word of God and needs to be stated and restated today. We are inclined to overlook this vital truth. Love of ease, spiritual laziness, and religious indifference all operate against this type of petitioning. Our praying, however, needs to be coaxed and pursued with an energy that never tires. It needs to have a persistency that will not be denied and a courage that never fails.

We also need to give thought to that mysterious fact of prayer—the certainty that there will be delays, denials, and seeming failures in connection with its exercise. We are to prepare for these and to permit them. However, we must not cease in our urgent praying. The praying Christian is like a brave soldier who, as the conflict grows more severe, exhibits a more superior courage than in the earlier stages of the battle. When delay and denial face him, he increases his earnest asking and does not stop until prayer prevails.

Moses furnished us with an excellent example of persistence in prayer. Instead of allowing his intimacy with God to release him from the necessity for persistence, he regarded it as something better to fit him for its exercise.

When Israel set up the golden calf, the wrath of God increased fiercely against them. Jehovah, bent on executing justice, said to Moses when He told him what He purposed to do, *"Let Me alone"* (Exodus 32:10; see also Deuteronomy 9:14–18). But Moses would not let Him alone. He threw himself down before the Lord in an agony of intercession on behalf of the sinning Israelites. For forty days and nights he fasted and prayed. What a season of persistent prayer that was!

Jehovah was also angry with Aaron, who had acted as leader in this idolatrous business of the golden calf. But Moses prayed for Aaron as well as for the Israelites. If he had not prayed, both Israel and Aaron would have perished under the consuming fire of God's wrath.

That long period of pleading before God left a mighty impression on Moses. He had been in close relationship with God before, but his character never attained the greatness that marked it in the days and years following this long season of persistent intercession.

There can be no question about persistent prayer moving God and heightening human character. If we were more in agreement with God in this great command of intercession, our faces would shine more brightly. Our lives and service would possess richer qualities that earn the goodwill of humanity and bring glory to the name of God.

14

PETITION

D. L. Moody

T he next element in prayer that I notice is petition. How often we go to prayer meetings without really asking for anything! Our prayers go all around the world, without anything definite being asked for. We do not expect anything. Many people would be greatly surprised if God did answer their prayers.

I remember hearing of a very eloquent man who was leading a meeting in prayer. There was not a single definite petition in his whole prayer. A poor, earnest woman shouted out, "Ask Him for something, man." How often you hear what is called prayer without any asking! *"Ask, and you shall receive"* (John 16:24).

I believe if we get all the stumbling blocks out of the way, God will answer our petitions. If we put away sin and come into His presence with pure hands, as He has commanded us to come, our prayers will have power with Him. In Luke's Gospel we have as a grand supplement to the Disciples' Prayer (see Luke 11:2–4) the following promise: *"Ask, and it shall be given you; seek, and you shall find; knock, and it shall be opened to you*" (Luke 11:9). Some people think God does not like to be troubled with our constant coming and asking. The only way to trouble God is not to come at all. He encourages us to come to Him repeatedly and press our claims.

I believe you will find three kinds of Christians in the church today. The first is those who ask; the second is those who seek; and the third is those who knock.

"Teacher," said a bright, earnest-faced boy, "why is it that so many prayers are unanswered? I do not understand. The Bible says, '*Ask, and it will be given to you; seek, and you will find; knock, and it will be opened to you*'; but it seems to me that many knock and are not admitted."

"Have you ever sat by your cheerful living room fire on some dark evening," said the teacher, "and heard a loud knock at the door? When you went to answer the door, did you peer out into the darkness, but saw nothing, yet you heard the pattering feet of some mischievous boy, who had knocked but did not wish to enter and so ran away? It is often thus with us. We ask for blessings but do not really expect them; we knock but do not plan to enter. We fear that Jesus will not hear us, will not fulfill His promises, will not admit us; and so we go away."

"Ah, I see," said the earnest-faced boy, his eyes shining with the new light dawning in his soul. "Jesus cannot be expected to answer runaway knocks. He has never promised it. I mean to keep knocking and knocking until He cannot help opening the door."

Too often we knock at mercy's door and then run away instead of waiting for an entrance and an answer. Thus, we act as if we were afraid of having our prayers answered.

Many people pray in that way; they do not wait for the answer. Our Lord is teaching us that we are not only to ask, but we are to wait for the answer. If it does not come, we must seek to find out the reason. I believe that we get a good number of blessings just by asking; others we do not get because there may be something in our lives that needs to be brought to light.

When Daniel began to pray in Babylon for the deliverance of his people, he sought to find out what the trouble was and why God had turned away His face from them. Likewise, there may be something in our lives that is keeping back the blessing; if there is, we need to find it.

Someone, speaking on this subject, has said, "We are to ask with a beggar's humility, to seek with a servant's carefulness, and to knock with the confidence of a friend."

How often people become discouraged and say they do not know whether God answers prayer! In the parable of the importunate widow (see Luke 18:2–8), Christ is teaching us how we are not only to pray and seek, but also to find. If the unjust judge heard the petition of the poor woman who pushed her claims, how much more will our heavenly Father hear our cry!

Many years ago in the state of New Jersey, an Irishman was condemned to be hanged. Every possible influence was brought to bear upon the governor to have the man reprieved, but he stood firm and refused to alter the sentence. One morning, the wife of the condemned man, with her ten children, went to see the governor. When he came to his office, they all fell on their faces before him and begged him to have mercy on the husband and father. The governor's heart was moved, and he at once wrote out a reprieve. The importunity of the wife and children saved the life of the man, just as the woman in the parable pressed her claims and induced the unjust judge to grant her request.

It was this same kind of persistence that brought the answer to the prayer of blind Bartimaeus. The people, and even the disciples, tried to hush him into silence; but he only cried out the louder, *"Son of David, have mercy on me"* (Mark 10:48).

Prayer is hardly ever mentioned in the Bible alone; it is prayer and earnestness, prayer and watchfulness, prayer and thanksgiving. We are instructed by the fact that, throughout Scripture, prayer is always linked with something else. Bartimaeus prayed earnestly, and the Lord heard his cry.

The highest type of Christian is the one who has gotten entirely beyond asking and seeking, and keeps on knocking until the answer comes. If we continue to knock, God has promised to open the door and grant our request. It may be years before the answer comes—He may keep us knocking—but He has promised that the answer will come.

I will tell you what I think it means to knock. A number of years ago, when we were having meetings in a certain city, it came to a point where there seemed to be very little power. We called together all the mothers and asked them to meet and pray for their children. About fifteen hundred mothers came together and poured out their hearts to God in prayer. One mother said, "I wish you would pray for my two boys. They have gone off on a drunken spree, and it seems as if my heart would break." She was a widowed mother. A few mothers gathered together and said, "Let us have a prayer meeting for these boys." They cried to God for these two wandering boys. Now see how God answered their prayer.

That day these two brothers had planned to meet at the corner of the street where our meetings were being held. They had planned to spend the night in debauchery and sin. About seven o'clock, the first one arrived at the appointed place; he saw people going into the meeting. Since it was a stormy night, he thought he would go in for a little while. The Word of God reached him, and he went into the inquiry room, where he gave his heart to the Savior.

The other brother waited at the corner until the meeting broke up, expecting his brother to come; he did not know that he had been in the meeting. There was another meeting for young men in the church nearby, and this brother thought he would like to see what was going on, so he followed the crowd into that meeting. He also was impressed with what he heard, and he was the first one to go into the inquiry room, where he found peace. While this was happening, the first one had gone home to cheer his mother's heart with the good news. He found her on her knees. She had been knocking at the mercy seat. While she was doing so, her boy came in and told her that her prayers had been answered;

his soul was saved. It was not long before the other brother came in and told his story how he, too, had been blessed.

On the following Monday night, the first to get up at the young converts' meeting was one of these brothers, who told the story of their conversion. No sooner had he taken his seat than the other jumped up and said, "All that my brother has told you is true, for I am his brother. The Lord has indeed met us and blessed us."

I heard of a certain wife in England who had an unconverted husband. She resolved that she would pray every day for twelve months for his conversion. Every day at twelve o'clock, she went to her room alone and cried to God. Her husband would not allow her to speak to him on the subject, but she could speak to God on his behalf. (It may be that you have a friend who does not wish to be spoken to about his salvation; you can do as this woman did—go and pray to God about it.)

The twelve months went by, and there was no sign of his yielding. She resolved to pray for six months longer; every day she went alone and prayed for the conversion of her husband. The six months passed, and still there was no sign, no answer. The question arose in her mind, "Can I give up on him?" "No," she vowed, "I will pray for him as long as God gives me breath."

That very day, when he came home to dinner, instead of going into the dining room, he went upstairs. She waited and waited, but he did not come down to dinner. Finally, she went to his room and found him on his knees, crying to God to have mercy upon him. God had convicted him of sin; he not only became a Christian, but the Word of God had free course and was glorified in him. (See 2 Thessalonians 3:1.) God used him mightily. That was God answering the prayers of this Christian wife; she knocked and knocked until the answer came.

I heard a story once that cheered me greatly. Prayer had been made for a man for about forty years, but there was no sign of any answer. It seemed as though he would go down to his grave as one of the most self-righteous men on the face of the earth. Conviction, however, came in one night. In the morning, he sent for the members of his family and said to his daughter, "I want you to pray for me. Pray that God would forgive my sins; my whole life has been nothing but sin—sin." This conviction came all at once in one night.

What we need to do is press our case right up to the throne of God. I have often known cases of men who came to our meetings, and although they could not hear a word that was said, it seemed as though some unseen power laid hold of them so that they were convicted and converted then and there.

I remember at one place where we were holding meetings, a wife came to the first meeting and asked me to talk with her husband. "He is not interested," she said, "but I have hope that he will become interested." I talked with him, and I think I have rarely ever spoken to a man who seemed so self-righteous. It looked as though I might as well have talked to an iron post, so encased he seemed to be in self-righteousness. I told his wife that he was not at all interested. She said, "I told you that, but I am interested for him."

All the thirty days we were there, that wife never gave up on him. I must confess she had ten times more faith for him than I had. I had spoken to him several times, but I could see no ray of hope. The third to last night, the man came to me and said, "Would you see me in another room?" I went aside with him and asked him what the trouble was. He said, "I am the greatest sinner in the state of Vermont." "How is that?" I asked. "Is there any particular sin you have been guilty of?" I must confess that I thought he had committed some awful crime that he had been covering up and that he now wanted to make confession.

"My whole life," he said, "has been nothing but sin. God has shown it to me today." He asked the Lord to have mercy on him, and he went home rejoicing in the assurance of sins forgiven. That was a man convicted and converted in answer to prayer.

If you are anxious about the conversion of some relative or friend, make up your mind that you will give God no rest, day or night, until He grants your petition. He can reach them, wherever they are—at their places of business, in their homes, or anywhere—and bring them to His feet.

Austin Phelps, in *The Still Hour*, said,

The prospect of gaining an object, will always affect thus the expression of intense desire.

The feeling which will become spontaneous with a Christian, under the influence of such a trust, is this: "I come to my devotions this morning, on an errand of real life. This is no romance and no farce. I do not come here to go through a form of words. I have no hopeless desires to express. I have an object to gain. I have an end to accomplish. This is a business in which I am about to engage. An astronomer does not turn his telescope to the skies with a more reasonable hope of penetrating those distant heavens, than I have of reaching the mind of God, by lifting up my heart at the throne of Grace. This is the privilege of my calling of God in Christ Jesus. Even my faltering voice is now to be heard in heaven, and it is to put forth a power there, the results of which only God can know, and only eternity can develop. Therefore, O Lord! thy servant findeth it in his heart to pray this prayer unto Thee."[11]

Jeremy Taylor said,

Indifferency and easiness of desire is a great enemy to the success of a good man's prayer. ...It must be an intent, zealous, busy, operative prayer; for, consider what a huge indecency it is, that a man should speak to God for a thing that he values not.... Our prayers upbraid our spirits, when we beg coldly and tamely for those things, for which we ought to die, which are more precious than the globes of kings, and weightier than imperial sceptres, richer than the spoils of the sea, or the treasures of Indian hills.[12]

---

11. Austin Phelps, *The Still Hour* (Boston: Gould and Lincoln, 1860), 42–43.
12. Jeremy Taylor, *The Whole Works of the Right Rev. Jeremy Taylor* (London: C. and J. Rivington, 1828), 71–73.

Dr. Patton, in his work *Prayer and Its Remarkable Answers*, illustrated the folly of praying without expecting to receive an answer:

> Jesus bids us "seek." Imagine a mother seeking a lost child. She looks through the house and along the streets, then searches the fields and woods, and examines the river-banks. A wise neighbor meets her and says: "Seek on; look everywhere; search every accessible place. You will not find, indeed; but then seeking is a good thing. It puts the mind on the stretch; it fixes the attention; it aids observation; it makes the idea of the child very real. And then, after a while, you will cease to want your child." The words of Christ are, "Knock." Imagine a man knocking at the door of a house, long and loud. After he has done this for an hour, a window opens, and the occupant of the house puts out his head, and says, "That is right, my friend; I shall not open the door, but then keep on knocking. It is excellent exercise, and you will be the healthier for it. Knock away till sundown; and then come again and knock all to-morrow. After some days thus spent, you will attain to a state of mind in which you will no longer care to come in." Is this what Jesus intended us to understand, when He said: "Ask, and ye shall receive; seek, and ye shall find; knock, and it shall be opened unto you"? No doubt one would thus soon cease to ask, to seek, and to knock; but would it not be from disgust?[13]

Nothing is more pleasing to our heavenly Father than direct, importunate, and persevering prayer. Two Christian ladies, whose husbands were unconverted, feeling their great danger, agreed to spend one hour each day in united prayer for their salvation. This was continued for seven years. At this time, they debated whether they should pray any longer, so useless did their prayers appear. They decided to persevere until death, and, if their husbands went to destruction, the way would be laden with prayers. In renewed strength, they prayed three years longer,

---

13. William Weston Patton, *Prayer and Its Remarkable Answers* (Chicago: J. S. Goodman, 1877), 42–43.

when one of them was awakened in the night by her husband, who was in great distress for sin. As soon as the day dawned, she hastened with joy to tell her praying companion that God was about to answer their prayers. Imagine her surprise to meet her friend coming to her on the same errand! Thus, ten years of united and persevering prayer was crowned with the conversion of both husbands on the same day.

We cannot be too frequent in our requests; God will not weary of His children's prayers. Sir Walter Raleigh asked a favor of Queen Elizabeth, to which she replied, "Raleigh, when will you leave off begging?" "When Your Majesty leaves off giving," he replied. That is how long we must continue praying.

In an address he gave in Calcutta, George Müller said that five people were laid on his heart in 1844, and he began to pray for them. Eighteen months went by before one of them was converted. He prayed on for five more years, and another was converted. At the end of twelve and a half years, a third was converted. In addition, he had been praying for the other two for forty years without missing one single day for any reason whatsoever, but they were not yet converted. He felt encouraged, however, to continue in prayer, and he was sure of receiving an answer in relation to the two who were still resisting the Spirit.

15

REAL PRAYER

Charles Spurgeon

Call upon Me in the day of trouble: I will deliver you, and you shall glorify Me. (Psalm 50:15)

One book charmed me when I was a boy. *Robinson Crusoe* was a wealth of wonders to me. I could have read it twenty times and never grown tired of it. I am not ashamed to confess that I can read it even now with ever fresh delight.

Robinson and his trusted aide Friday, though mere inventions of fiction, are wonderfully real to me, as they are to the many who have read their story. But why am I going on and on about a work of fiction? Is this subject altogether out of place? I hope not. A passage in that book comes vividly to my mind as I contemplate our text, and in it I find more than an excuse to write on this subject.

Robinson Crusoe had been shipwrecked. All alone on a desert island, he was in a very miserable condition. He went to bed and was afflicted with a fever. This fever lasted a long time, and he had no one to help him—no one even to bring him a drink of cold water. He was ready to die.

He was accustomed to sin and had all the vices of an evil sailor, but his hard case caused him to think. Opening a Bible that he had found in his sea chest, he stumbled upon this passage: "*Call upon Me in the day of trouble: I will deliver you, and you shall glorify Me.*" That night he prayed for the first time in his life, and ever after that, he had a hope in God.

Daniel Defoe, the author of the book, was a Presbyterian minister. Though not overly spiritual, he knew enough of faith to be able to describe very vividly the experience of a person who is in despair but finds peace by casting himself upon God. As a novelist, he had a keen eye for the probable, and he could think of no passage more likely to impress a poor broken spirit than this. Instinctively, he perceived the wealth of comfort that lies within the words of Psalm 50:15.

Now I know I have your attention, and that is one reason that I began the chapter this way. But I have a further purpose. Although Robinson Crusoe was not a real person, nor was Friday either, there may be some reader very much like him, a person who has suffered shipwreck in life and has now become a drifting, solitary creature. He remembers better days, but by his sins he has become a castaway for whom no one seeks. He is reading this book, washed up on shore without a friend, suffering in body and crushed in spirit. In a city full of people, he does not have a friend. There is no one who would wish to admit that he has ever known him. He has come to the bare bones of existence now. Nothing lies before him but poverty, misery, and death.

The Lord says to you, my friend, "*Call upon Me in the day of trouble: I will deliver you, and you shall glorify Me.*" I have the feeling that I am writing directly, God helping me, to some poor burdened spirit. Of what use is comfort to those who are not in distress? The words of this chapter will be of no help and may have little interest to those who have no distress of heart. But, however badly I may write, those hearts that need the cheering assurance of a gracious God will dance for joy. Sad hearts will be enabled to receive assurance as it shines forth in this golden text: "*Call upon Me in the day of trouble: I will deliver you, and you shall glorify Me.*"

It is a text that I want to write in stars across the sky or proclaim with the blowing of a trumpet from the top of every tower. It should be known and read by all mankind.

Four important concepts suggest themselves to me. May the Holy Spirit bless what I am able to write about them!

BEING REAL BEFORE GOD

My first observation is not so much in my text alone as it is in the context. The observation is this: God prefers realism to ritualism. If you will carefully read the entire psalm, you will see that the Lord is speaking of the rituals and ceremonies of Israel. He is showing that He cares little about formalities of worship when the heart is absent from them. Here are several key verses that illustrate this:

I will not reprove you for your sacrifices or your burned offerings, to have been continually before Me. I will take no bullock out of your house, nor he goats out of your folds. For every beast of the forest is Mine, and the cattle upon a thousand hills. I know all the fowls of the mountains: and the wild beasts of the field are Mine. If I were hungry, I would not tell you: for the world is Mine, and the fullness thereof. Will I eat the flesh of bulls, or drink the blood of goats? Offer to God thanksgiving; and pay your vows to the Most High: and call upon Me in the day of trouble: I will deliver you, and you shall glorify Me. (Psalm 50:8–15)

Thus, praise and prayer are accepted in preference to every form of offering that the Jew could possibly present before the Lord. Why is this?

REAL PRAYER HAS MEANING

First of all, real prayer is far better than mere ritual because there is meaning in it. When grace is absent, there is no meaning in ritual. It is as senseless as a fool's game.

Did you ever stand in a Roman Catholic cathedral and watch the daily service, especially if it happened to be on a holiday? With the boys in white, and the men in violet, pink, red, or black, there are enough performers to entertain a city. There are those who carry candlesticks, those who carry crosses, those who carry cushions and books, those who ring bells, those who sprinkle water, those who bob their heads, and those who bow their knees. The whole scene is very strange to look at—very amazing, very amusing, very childish. One wonders, when he sees it, what it is all about, and what kind of people are really made better by it. One wonders also what an idea Roman Catholics must have of God if they imagine that He is pleased with such performances. Do you not wonder how the Lord endures it? What must His glorious mind think of it all?

The glorious God cares nothing for pomp and show. But when you call upon Him in the day of trouble and ask Him to deliver you, there is meaning in your groan of anguish. This is no empty formality. There is heart in it, is there not? There is meaning in the sorrowful appeal. Therefore, God prefers the prayer of a broken heart to the finest service that was ever performed by priests and choirs.

REAL PRAYER HAS SPIRITUAL LIFE

Why does God prefer realism to ritualism? It is for this reason also: There is something spiritual in the cry of a troubled heart. *"God is a Spirit: and they that worship Him must worship Him in spirit and in truth"* (John 4:24). Suppose I were to repeat the finest creed that was ever composed by learned and orthodox men. Yet, if I had no faith in it, and you had none, what would be the use of repeating the words? There is nothing spiritual in mere orthodox statements if we have no real belief in them. We might as well repeat the alphabet and call it devotion. If I were to burst forth in the grandest hallelujah that was ever uttered by mortal lips, but I did not mean it, there would be nothing spiritual in it, and it would mean nothing to God.

However, when a poor soul gets away into his bedroom and bows his knee and cries, "God be merciful to me! God save me! God help me in this day of trouble!" there is spiritual life in such a cry. Therefore,

God approves it and answers it. Spiritual worship is what He wants, and He will have it or have nothing. John 4:24 uses the word *must*: *"They that worship Him must worship Him in spirit and in truth."* He has abolished the ceremonial law, destroyed the one altar at Jerusalem, burned the temple, abolished the Aaronic priesthood, and ended forever all ritualistic performance. He seeks only true worshipers, who worship Him in spirit and in truth.

REAL PRAYER RECOGNIZES GOD

Furthermore, the Lord loves the cry of the broken heart because it distinctly recognizes Him as the living God, truly sought after in prayer. From much of outward devotion God is absent. But how we mock God when we do not discern Him as present and do not come near to the Lord Himself! When the heart or the mind or the soul breaks through itself to get to its God, then God is glorified. But He is not glorified when we merely perform ritualistic exercises and forget about Him. Oh, how real God is to a person who is perishing and feels that only God can save him! He truly believes that God exists, or else he would not make so passionate a prayer to Him. When he said his prayers before, he cared little whether God heard or not. But he genuinely prays now, and God's hearing is his chief concern.

REAL PRAYER HAS SINCERITY

In addition, dear friends, God takes great delight in our crying to Him in the day of trouble because there is sincerity in it. I am afraid that in the hour of our mirth and in the day of our prosperity, many of our prayers and our thanksgivings are hypocrisy. Too many of us are like spinning tops—we do not move into action unless we are whipped. Certainly we pray with deep intensity when we get into deep trouble.

Take, for instance, a man who is very poor. He has lost his job. He has worn out his shoes in trying to find work. He does not know where the next meal is coming from for his children. If he prays in this situation, it is likely to be a very sincere prayer. He would be in real earnest because of real trouble.

I have sometimes wished that very comfortable Christians, who seem to treat religion as if it were a bed of roses, could have just a little time of "roughing it" and really come into actual difficulties. A life of ease breeds hosts of falsehoods and pretenses, which would soon vanish in the presence of matter-of-fact trials.

MANY A MAN HAS BEEN CONVERTED TO GOD BY HUNGER, WEARINESS, AND LONELINESS, WHO, WHEN HE WAS A WEALTHY MAN, SURROUNDED BY FRIVOLOUS FLATTERERS, NEVER THOUGHT OF GOD AT ALL.

Many a man has been converted to God by hunger, weariness, and loneliness, who, when he was a wealthy man, surrounded by frivolous flatterers, never thought of God at all. Many a man on board a ship out on the ocean has learned to pray in the cold chill of an iceberg, or in the horrors of a tidal wave out of which the ship could not rise. When the mast has gone by the board and every timber has been strained and the ship has seemed doomed, then hearts have begun to pray in sincerity.

God loves sincerity. When we mean it; when the soul melts in prayer; when we say, "I must have it or be lost;" when it is no sham, no vain performance, but a real heartbreaking, agonizing cry, then God accepts it. That is why He says, *Call upon Me in the day of trouble.* Such a cry is the kind of worship that He cares for, because there is sincerity in it, and this is acceptable with the God of truth.

REAL PRAYER HAS HUMILITY

Furthermore, in the cry of the troubled one, there is humility. We may go through a highly brilliant performance of religion, following the rites of some showy church—or we may go through our own rites, which may be as simple as they can be—and we may all the while be saying to ourselves, "This is very nicely done." The preacher may be thinking, "Am I not preaching well?" The believer at the prayer meeting may think within himself, "How delightfully fluent I am!" Whenever there is that attitude in us, God cannot accept our worship. Worship is not acceptable if it is devoid of humility.

On the other hand, when a person goes to God in the day of trouble and says, "Lord, help me! I cannot help myself, but do intervene for me," there is humility in that confession and cry. Therefore, the Lord takes delight in that prayer.

REAL PRAYER HAS FAITH

The Lord loves such pleadings because there is a measure of faith in them. When the person in trouble cries, "Lord, deliver me!" he is looking away from himself. You see, he is driven out of himself because of the despair in his life. He cannot find hope or help on earth, and therefore he looks toward heaven.

God loves to discover even a shadow of faith in an unbelieving person. God can spy out even a small trace of faith, and He can and will accept prayer for the sake of that little faith.

Oh, dear heart, what is your condition? Are you torn with anguish? Are you sorely distressed? Are you lonely? Are you pushed aside? Then cry to God. No one else can help you. He is your only hope. Wonderful hope! Cry to Him, for He can help you. I tell you, in that cry of yours will be the pure and true worship that God desires. He desires a sincere cry far more than the slaughter of thousands of rams or the pouring out of ten thousand rivers of oil. (See Micah 6:7.) We undoubtedly find in Scripture that the groan of a burdened spirit is among the sweetest sounds that are ever heard by the ear of the Most High. Woeful cries are anthems with Him, to whom all mere arrangements of sound must be like child's play.

See then, poor, weeping, and distracted ones, that it is not ritualism, it is not the performance of pompous ceremonies, it is not bowing and struggling, it is not using sacred words, but it is crying to God in the hour of trouble that is the most acceptable sacrifice your spirit can bring before the throne of God.

HOW TO TAKE ADVANTAGE OF ADVERSITY

I now come to my second observation. In our text, *"Call upon Me in the day of trouble: I will deliver you,"* we have adversity turned into advantage. What a wonderful truth! May God impress it on us all!

I write this with all reverence: God Himself cannot deliver a person who is not in trouble. Therefore, it is to some advantage to be in distress, because God can then deliver you. Even Jesus Christ, the Healer of men, cannot heal a person who is not sick. Therefore, sickness is not an adversity for us, but rather an advantageous opportunity for Christ to heal us.

The point is, my reader, your adversity may prove your advantage by offering occasion for the display of divine grace. It is wise to learn the art of making lemonade out of lemons, and the text teaches us how to do that. It shows how trouble can become gain. When you are in adversity, then call upon God, and you will experience a deliverance that will be a richer and sweeter experience for your soul than if you had never known trouble. It is an art and a science to make gains out of losses, and advantages out of adversities.

Now, let me suppose that there is someone among my readers who is in trouble—perhaps another deserted Robinson Crusoe. I am not idly supposing that there is a tried individual among my readership; I know there is.

Well now, when you pray—and, oh, I wish you would pray now— do you not see what a basis for prayer you have? First, you have a basis in the very time you are in: *"the day of trouble."* You can plead, "Lord, this is a day of trouble! I am in great affliction, and my case is urgent!" Then state what your trouble is—a sick wife, a dying child, a bankrupt business, your failing health, or poverty staring you in the face. Say unto the Lord of mercy, "My Lord, if ever a person was in a day of trouble, I am. Therefore, I take the liberty and license to pray to You now because You have said, '*Call upon Me in the day of trouble.*' This is the hour that You have appointed for appealing to You: this dark, stormy day. If ever there were a person who had a right to pray according to Your own Word, I do, for I am in trouble. Therefore, I will make use of the very time I am in as a plea with You. Do, I entreat You, hear Your servant's cry in this midnight hour."

Furthermore, turn your adversity into advantage by pleading God's command. You can go to the Lord now, at this precise instant, and say, "Lord, do hear me, for You have commanded me to pray! I, though I am evil, would not tell someone to ask me for something if I intended to deny him. I would not urge him to ask for help if I meant to refuse it."

Do you not know, friends, that we often impute to the Lord conduct that we would be ashamed of in ourselves? This must not be. Suppose you said to a poor person, "You are in very sad circumstances. Write to me tomorrow, and I will help you." If he did write to you, you would not treat his letter with contempt. You would be bound to consider his case. When you told him to write, you meant that you would help him if you could. And when God tells you to call upon Him, He does not mock you. He means that He will deal kindly with you.

I do not know who you are, but you may call upon the Lord, for He bids you to call. If you do call upon Him, you can put this argument into your prayer:

Hast Thou not bid me seek Thy face,
And shall I seek in vain?
And shall the ear of sovereign grace,
Be deaf when I complain?

So, plead the time, plead the trouble, and plead the command. Then, plead God's own character. Speak with Him reverently, but believingly, in this fashion: "Lord, it is You Yourself to whom I appeal. You have said, '*Call upon Me.*' If my neighbor would tell me to do so, I might fear that perhaps he would change his mind and not hear me. But You are too great and too good to change. Lord, by Your truth and by Your faithfulness, by Your immutability and by Your love, I, a poor sinner, heartbroken and crushed, call upon You in the day of trouble! Oh, help me, and help me soon, or else I will die!"

Surely you who are in trouble have many and mighty pleas. You are on firm ground with the God of the covenant, and you may bravely seize the blessing. I do not feel as if the text is encouraging me half as much as it will encourage those of my readers who are in trouble. Although I thank God that I am full of joy and rest right now, I am half inclined to see if I can dig up a little bit of trouble for myself. Surely if I were in trouble, I would open my mouth and drink in this text. I would pray like David or Elijah or Daniel with the power of this promise: *"Call upon Me in the day of trouble: I will deliver you, and you shall glorify Me."*

Oh, you troubled ones, leap up at the sound of this promise! Believe it. Let it go down into your souls. *"The LORD loosens the prisoners"* (Psalm 146:7). He has come to free you.

I can see my Master arrayed in His silk garments. His countenance is as joyous as heaven, His face is as bright as a morning without clouds, and in His hand He holds a silver key. "Where are you going, my Master, with that silver key of Yours?" I ask. "I go," He says, "to open the door of the captive and to loosen everyone who is bound."

Blessed Master, fulfill Your errand, but do not pass by the prisoners of hope! We will not hinder You for a moment, but do not forget these mourners! Go to the heart of every reader, and set free the prisoners of despair. Make their hearts sing for joy by delivering them in the day of trouble after they have called upon You. Because of Your merciful deliverance, they will glorify You!

GOD PROMISES GRACE

My third topic, God's vow, is clearly found in our text, Psalm 50:15. Here we have free grace vowed to us.

Nothing in heaven or earth can be freer than grace. In our wonderful text God's grace is promised by a vow or covenant. Listen to God's definite promise to deliver us: *"Call upon Me in the day of trouble: I will deliver you."*

If a person once says to you, "I will," you hold him to his promise. He has placed himself at the command of his own declaration. If he is a true man and has plainly said, "I will," you have him in your hand. He was free before giving the promise, but he is not free after giving it. He has put himself in a certain position, and he must act according to what he has promised. Is this not true?

With the deepest reverence, I say the same things about my Lord and Master. He has bound Himself in the text with cords that He will not break. He must now hear and help those who call upon Him in the day of trouble. He has solemnly promised, and He will fully perform His vow.

Notice that our text is unconditional in that it applies to everyone. It contains the gist of another promise: *"whosoever shall call upon the name of the Lord shall be saved"* (Romans 10:13).

Remarkably, Psalm 50:15 was originally written to those who had mocked God. They had presented their sacrifices without a true heart. Yet, the Lord said to each of them, *"Call upon Me in the day of trouble: I will deliver you."*

I gather from this that God excludes none from the promise. You atheist, you blasphemer, you immoral and impure one, if you call upon the Lord now, in the day of your trouble, He will deliver you! Come and try Him.

Do you say, "If there is a God"? I declare that there is a God. Come, put Him to the test and see. He says, *"Call upon Me in the day of trouble: I will deliver you."* Will you not test Him now and find Him true? Come here, you enslaved ones, and see if He does not free you! Come to Christ, all of you who labor and are burdened down, and He will give you rest! (See Matthew 11:28.) In both temporal and spiritual things, but especially in spiritual things, call upon Him in the day of trouble, and He will deliver you.

Moreover, notice that this "I will" includes all the power that may be required for deliverance. "*Call upon Me in the day of trouble: I will deliver you.*" "But how can this be?" one cries. Ah, that I cannot tell you, and I do not feel bound to tell you. It rests with the Lord to find suitable ways and means. God says, "*I will.*" Let Him do it in His own way. If He says, "*I will,*" you can be sure that He will keep His word. If it is necessary to shake heaven and earth, He will do it. He cannot lack power, and He certainly does not lack honesty. An honest man will keep his word at all costs, and so will our faithful God. Hear Him say, "*I will deliver you,*" and ask no more questions.

I do not suppose that Daniel knew how God would deliver him out of the den of lions. I do not suppose that Joseph knew how he would be delivered out of prison when his master's wife had slandered his character so shamefully. I do not suppose that these ancient believers even dreamed of the way of the Lord's deliverance. They just left themselves in God's hands. They rested on God, and He delivered them in the best possible manner. He will do the same for you. Simply call upon Him, and then "*stand still, and see the salvation of the LORD*" (Exodus 14:13).

Notice, the text does not say exactly when God will bring deliverance. "*I will deliver you*" is plain enough, but whether it will be tomorrow or next week or next year is not so clear. You are in a great hurry, but the Lord is not. Your trial may not have yet worked all the good for you that it was sent to do, and therefore it must last longer. When the gold is cast into the refiner's fire, it might cry to the goldsmith, "Let me out." "No," he says, "you have not yet lost your dross. You must wait in the fire until I have purified you."

God may likewise subject us to many trials. Yet, if He says, "*I will deliver you,*" you can be sure that He will keep His word. When you get God's "*I will,*" you may always cash it by faith. God's promise for the future is a bona fide offer for the present, if you simply have faith to use it. "*Call upon Me in the day of trouble: I will deliver you*" is tantamount to deliverance already received. It means, "If I do not deliver you now, I will deliver you at a time that is better than now. You would prefer to be delivered at this future time rather than now if you were as wise as I am."

Promptness is implied in God's promise of deliverance, for a late deliverance is not truly deliverance. "Ah," someone says, "I am in such trouble that if I do not get deliverance soon I will die of grief." Rest assured that you will not die of despair. You will be delivered before you die that way. God will deliver you at the best possible time.

The Lord is always punctual. You never were kept waiting by Him. You have kept Him waiting many times, but He is prompt to the instant. He never keeps His servants waiting one single tick of the clock beyond His own appointed, fitting, wise, and proper moment. *"I will deliver you"* implies that His delays will not be too long, lest the spirit of man should fail because of hope deferred. The Lord rides on the wings of the wind when He comes to the rescue of those who seek Him. Therefore, be courageous!

Oh, this is a blessed text! But, unfortunately, I cannot carry it to those of you who need it most. Spirit of the living God, come, and apply these rich consolations to those hearts that are bleeding and ready to die!

As I repeat our text, take special note of the words *I* and *you*: *"Call upon Me in the day of trouble: I will deliver you."* Those two words are threaded together: *"I will deliver you."* Men would not, angels could not, but God will. God Himself will rescue the person who calls upon Him. Your part is to call; God's part is to answer. Poor trembler, do you begin to try to answer your own prayers? Why did you pray to God then? When you have prayed, leave it to God to fulfill His own promise. He says, "Do call upon Me, and I will deliver you."

GOD HIMSELF WILL RESCUE THE PERSON WHO
CALL UPON HIM. YOUR PART IS TO CALL;
GOD'S PART IS TO ANSWER.

Especially ponder that word you: *"I will deliver you."* I know what you are thinking, reader. You murmur, "God will deliver everybody, I believe, but *not me*." But the text says, *"I will deliver you."* It is the person who calls who will get the answer. If you call upon God, He will answer you. To you He will give the blessing, even to your own heart and spirit, in your own experience. Oh, for grace to take that personal pronoun and apply it personally to our own souls! Oh, to make sure of the promise as though we could see it with our own eyes!

The apostle wrote, *"Through faith we understand that the worlds were framed by the word of God"* (Hebrews 11:3). I know beyond the shadow of a doubt that the worlds were made by God. I am sure of it. Yet I did not see Him making them. I did not see the light appear when He said, *"Let there be light"* (Genesis 1:3). I did not see Him divide the light from the darkness and gather the waters together so that the dry land appeared. Yet I am quite sure that He did all this. Even though I was not there to see God make even a bird or a flower, all the evolutionists in the world cannot shake my conviction that God created the world.

Why should I not have the same kind of faith about God's answer to my prayer in my time of trouble? If I cannot see how He will deliver me, why should I wish to see it? He created the world well enough without me being there and knowing how He would do it, and He will deliver me without my having a finger in it. It is no business of mine to see how He works. My business is to trust in my God and to glorify Him by believing that what He has promised, He is able to perform. (See Romans 4:21.)

TAKING TURNS WITH GOD

We have had three sweet things to remember, and I will close this chapter with a fourth. It is this: both God and the praying person have parts to play in this process.

That is an odd idea to close with, but I want you to notice it. First, here is your part: *"Call upon Me in the day of trouble."* Next is God's part: *"I will deliver you."* Again, you take another part in that you are delivered and in that you praise Him for it: *"You shall glorify Me."* Then, the Lord takes the last part in that He receives the glory. Here is an agreement, a covenant that God enters into with those who pray to Him and are helped by Him. He says, "You will have the deliverance, but I must have the glory. You will pray, I will bless, and then you will honor My holy name." Here is a delightful partnership: we obtain what we so greatly need, and all that God asks is the glory that is due unto His name.

Poor troubled heart! I am sure you do not object to these terms. "Sinners," says the Lord, "I will give you pardon, but you must give Me the honor for it." Our only answer is, "Yes, Lord, that we will, forever and ever."

> Who is a pard'ning God like Thee?
> Or who has grace so rich and free?

"Come, souls," He says, "I will justify you, but I must have the glory for it." And our answer is, *"Where is boasting then? It is excluded. By what law? of works? Nay: but by the law of faith"* (Romans 3:27). God must have the glory if we are justified by Christ.

"Come," He says, "I will put you into My family, but My grace must have all the glory." And we say, "Yes, that it will, good Lord! *'Behold, what manner of love the Father has bestowed upon us, that we should be called the sons of God'* (1 John 3:1)."

"Now," He says, "I will sanctify you and make you holy, but I must have the glory for it." And our answer is, "Yes, we will sing this song forever: 'We have washed our robes and made them white in the blood of the Lamb. (See Revelation 7:14) Therefore, we will serve Him day and night in His temple, giving Him all praise.'"

"I will take you home to heaven," God says. "I will deliver you from sin and death and hell, but I must have the glory for it." "Truly," we say, "You will be magnified. Forever and forever we will sing, *'Blessing, and honor, and glory, and power, be to Him that sits upon the throne, and to the Lamb for ever and ever'* (Revelation 5:13)."

Stop, you thief! Where are you going? Running away with a portion of God's glory? A person who would steal God's glory must be quite a villain! Take, for example, a man who was recently an alcoholic. God has loved him and made him sober, but he takes the credit and is extremely proud of his sobriety. What foolishness! Stop it, mister! Stop it! Give God the glory for your deliverance from the degrading vice, or else you are still degraded by ingratitude.

Take another man as an example. He used to swear, but he has been praying now. He even delivered a sermon the other night, or at least a personal testimony. He has been as proud as a peacock about this. Oh, bird of pride, when you look at your fine feathers, remember your black feet and your hideous voice! Oh, reclaimed sinner, remember your former character, and be ashamed! Give God the glory if you have ceased to use profane language. Give God the glory for every part of your salvation.

"I will deliver you"—that is your share to receive. But, *"You shall glorify Me"*—that is God's share, and His only. He must have all the honor from first to last.

Go out, you saved ones, and proclaim what the Lord has done for you. An aged woman once said that if the Lord Jesus Christ really would save her, He would never hear the last of her praise. Join with her in that resolution. Truly, my soul vows that my delivering Lord will never hear the last of my praise.

> I'll praise Him in life, and praise Him in death,
> And praise Him as long as He lendeth me breath,
> And say when the deathdew lies cold on my brow:
> If ever I loved Thee, my Jesus, 'tis now.

Come, poor soul, you who are in the deepest of trouble—God means to glorify Himself by you! The day will yet come when you will comfort other mourners by telling your happy experience. The day will yet come when you who were outcasts will preach the gospel to outcasts. The day will yet come, poor fallen woman, when you will lead other sinners to the Savior's feet where you now stand weeping! You, who have been abandoned by the devil, whom even Satan is tired of, whom the world rejects because you are worn out and stale—the day will yet come when, renewed in heart and washed in the blood of the Lamb, you will shine like a star in the sky, to the praise of the glory of the grace of God, who has made you to be accepted in the Beloved! (See Ephesians 1:6.)

Oh, despondent sinner, come to Jesus! Do call upon Him, I entreat you! Be persuaded to call upon your God and Father. If you can do no more than groan, groan unto God. Drop a tear, heave a sigh, and let your heart say to the Lord, "O God, deliver me for Christ's sake! Save me from my sin and the consequences of it." As surely as you pray this way, He will hear you and say, "Your sins are forgiven. Go in peace." May it be so for you today, my friend.

16

PROVING THE ACCEPTABLE WILL OF GOD

George Müller

(It is very instructive and helpful to see the way in which Müller proved the acceptable will of the Lord when his heart was opened to pursue the enlargement of the orphan work, so that not only three hundred but one thousand orphans might be provided for.)

December 11, 1850. The specific burden of my prayer is that God would be pleased to teach me His will. My mind has also been especially pondering how I could know His will satisfactorily concerning this specific request. I am sure that I will be taught. I therefore desire patiently for the Lord's time, when He will be pleased to shine on my path concerning this point.

GOD'S CALM ASSURANCE

December 26. Fifteen days have elapsed since I wrote the preceding paragraph. Every day since then, I have continued to pray about this matter, and that with a considerable measure of earnestness, by the help of God. Scarcely an hour has passed during these days, in which, while awake, this matter has not been more or less before me. But all without even a shadow of excitement. I converse with no one about it. To this point, I have not even done so with my dear wife. I still refrain from discussing it with others and deal with God alone about the matter, in order that no outward influence, and no outward excitement, may keep me from attaining a clear discovery of God's will.

I have the fullest and most peaceful assurance that He will clearly show me His will. This evening I have had again an especially solemn season of prayer to seek to know the will of God. But while I continue to entreat and beseech the Lord that He would not allow me to be deluded in this business, I may say I have scarcely any doubt remaining in my mind as to what will be the result, even that I should go forward in this matter.

As this, however, is one of the most momentous steps that I have ever taken, I judge that I cannot go about this matter with too much caution, prayer, and deliberation. I am in no hurry about it. I could wait for years, by God's grace, were this His will, before even taking one single step toward this thing, or even speaking to anyone about it; on the other hand, I would set to work tomorrow were the Lord to bid me to do so.

This calmness of mind, this having no will of my own in the matter, this only wishing to please my heavenly Father in it, this only seeking His and not my honor in it, this state of heart, I say, is the fullest assurance to me that my heart is not under a fleshly excitement, and that, if I am helped thus to go on, I will know the will of God fully. But, while I write thus, I cannot but add at the same time that I do crave the honor and the glorious privilege to be more and more used by the Lord. I served Satan much in my younger years, and I desire now with all my might to serve God during the remaining days of my earthly pilgrimage.

I am forty-five years and three months old. Every day decreases the number of days that I have to stay on earth. I therefore desire with all my might to work. Vast multitudes of orphans need to be provided for.

I desire that it may be yet more abundantly made clear that God is still the hearer and answerer of prayer and that He is the living God now—as He ever was and ever will be—when He will, simply in answer to prayer, have condescended to provide me with a house for seven hundred orphans and the means to support them. This last consideration is the most important point in my mind. The Lord's honor is the principal point with me in this whole matter; and just because that is the case, if He would be more glorified by my not going forward in this business, I would, by His grace, be perfectly content to give up all thoughts about another orphanage. Surely in such a state of mind, obtained by the Holy Spirit, You, O my heavenly Father, will not allow your child to be mistaken, much less to be deluded. By the help of God, I will continue further, day by day, to wait upon Him in prayer concerning this thing, until He directs me to act.

TRUST IN THE LORD

January 2, 1851. I wrote the preceding paragraph a week ago. During this week, I have still been helped, day by day, and more than once every day, to seek the guidance of the Lord about another orphanage. The burden of my prayer has still been that He, in His great mercy, would keep me from making a mistake. During the last week, the book of Proverbs has come in the course of my Scripture reading, and my heart has been refreshed, in reference to this subject, by the following passages: *"Trust in the LORD with all your heart; and lean not to your own understanding. In all your ways acknowledge Him, and He shall direct your paths"* (Proverbs 3:5–6).

By the grace of God, I do acknowledge the Lord in all my ways, and in this thing in particular. I have therefore the comfortable assurance that He will direct my paths concerning this part of my service, as to whether I will be occupied in it or not. Further, *"the integrity of the upright shall guide them: but the perverseness of transgressors shall destroy them"* (Proverbs 11:3). By the grace of God, I am upright in this business. My holiest purpose is to give glory to God. Therefore I expect to be guided aright.

The Scriptures also say, *"Commit your works to the LORD, and your thoughts shall be established"* (Proverbs 16:3). I do commit my works to the Lord; therefore, I expect that my thoughts will be established. My heart is more and more coming to a calm, quiet, and settled assurance that the Lord will condescend to use me yet further in the orphan work. "Here, Lord, is Your servant!" (See 1 Samuel 3:9–10; Isaiah 6:8.)

A PEACEFUL DECISION

(Müller wrote down eight reasons against and eight reasons for establishing another orphanage for seven hundred orphans. The following was his last reason for going ahead with the project.)

I am peaceful and happy, spiritually, in the prospect of enlarging the work, as on former occasions when I was led to do so. This weighs particularly with me as a reason for going forward. After all the calm, quiet, prayerful consideration of the subject for about eight weeks, I am peaceful and happy, spiritually, in the purpose of enlarging the work. This, after all the heart-searching that I have had, and the daily prayer to be kept from delusion and mistake in this thing, and the faithful reading of the Word of God, would not be the case, I judge, if the Lord had not purposed to condescend to use me more than ever in His service.

I, therefore, on the grounds that the objections have been answered, and that these eight reasons for enlarging the work remain, come to the conclusion that it is the will of the blessed God that I, His poor and most unworthy servant, should yet more extensively serve Him in this work, which I am quite willing to do.

May 24. From the time that I began to write down the thoughts of my mind on December 5, 1850, until this day, ninety-two more applications for orphans needing homes have been received, and seventy-eight were already waiting for admission before. But this number increases rapidly as the work becomes more and more known.

On the basis of what has been recorded above, I purpose to go forward in this service, and to seek to build, to the praise and honor of the living God, another orphanage, large enough to accommodate seven hundred orphans.

17

PRAYING IN THE NAME OF JESUS CHRIST

R. A. Torrey

And whatsoever you shall ask in My name, that will I do, that the Father may be glorified in the Son. If you shall ask any thing in My name, I will do it. (John 14:13–14)

This is one of the most familiar, most wonderful, and at the same time most commonly misunderstood promises in the Bible regarding God's willingness to answer prayer.

Here our Lord Jesus Christ Himself tells us that if a certain class of people pray in a certain way, He will give them the very thing that they ask. Look at the promise again. These words are plain, simple, positive, very precious, and cheering. They tell us that there are certain people who can get from God anything that they ask for, if only they will ask for it in a certain way.

There is a doctrine regarding prayer that is very common in our day. It is this: "If we pray, our praying will do much good in many ways. We may not get the very thing that we ask, but we will get something, something just as good as what we ask, or perhaps something far better than what we ask." I do not doubt that there is a measure of truth in this doctrine. It is a good thing sometimes that some of us do not get what we ask for; we are so careless, thoughtless, hasty, and so little under the control of the Holy Spirit when we pray, that it is oftentimes a good thing for us, and a good thing for others, that we do not get the very thing that we ask. It would be a great misfortune if some of us got some of the things that we ask of God. But while there is a certain measure of truth in that doctrine, it is not the doctrine of prayer taught in the Bible.

The doctrine of prayer taught in the Bible is that there are certain people who can pray in a certain way and who will get not merely some good thing, or something just as good as what they ask, or something even better than what they ask, but the very thing that they ask. *"And whatsoever you shall ask in My name, that will I do, that the Father may be glorified in the Son. If you shall ask any thing in My name, I will do it."* There are two things to notice about this promise: first, to whom the promise is made, and who can ask in the name of the Lord Jesus and get the very thing they ask; second, how these persons must pray in order to get what they ask.

TO WHOM THE PROMISE IS MADE

First of all, notice to whom this promise is made. One of the most common sources of misinterpretation of the Bible is the applying of promises that are made to a certain clearly defined class of people to whom the promises were never made. God does not promise to answer the prayers of everyone; indeed, He tells us plainly that there are people whose prayers He will pay no attention whatsoever. In the case of the present promise, we are told very definitely in the context just whose prayers God will answer, if they are offered in a certain way. Who are the people to whom God says through His Son Jesus Christ, *"And whatsoever you shall ask in My name, that will I do"*? They are clearly described in verse twelve, the verse that immediately precedes, and verses fifteen and seventeen, the verses that follow the promise.

THOSE WHO BELIEVE ON JESUS CHRIST

First of all, then, look at verse twelve: *"Verily, verily, I say to you, he that believes on Me, the works that I do shall he do also; and greater works than these shall he do; because I go to My Father."* And then our Lord goes on to say, *"And whatsoever you* [that is, you who believe on the Son, as just defined] *shall ask in my name, that will I do."* The promise is therefore made, first of all, to those who believe on Jesus Christ. Notice that it is not made to those who believe *about* Jesus Christ, but those who believe *on* Jesus Christ. People are constantly confusing in their own minds two entirely different things—believing about Jesus Christ and believing on Jesus Christ. God does not promise to answer the prayers of those who merely believe about Jesus Christ even though their faith is perfectly and rigidly orthodox. He does promise to answer the prayers of those who believe on Jesus Christ. A person may believe perfectly correctly about Jesus Christ, and yet not believe on Him at all. The devil himself believes about Jesus Christ, and is undoubtedly perfectly orthodox; he knows more about Jesus Christ as He really is than we do, but the devil certainly does not believe on Jesus Christ. There are many today who, because their view of Jesus Christ is perfectly orthodox, imagine that they believe on Jesus Christ. But that does not logically follow at all.

What does it mean to believe on Jesus Christ? To believe on Jesus Christ means to put our personal confidence in Jesus Christ as what He claims to be, and to accept Him to be to us what He offers Himself to be. It means that we accept Him as our Savior, as the One who *"bore our sins in His own body on the tree"* (1 Peter 2:24). It means that we trust God to forgive us because Jesus Christ died in our place, and also that we accept Him as our Lord and Master to whom we surrender the absolute control of our lives. This we are told in so many words in John 1:12: *"But as many as received Him, to them gave He power to become the sons of God, even to them that believe on His name."*

Nowhere in the entire Bible does God promise to hear the prayers of people who do not believe on Jesus Christ; that is, the prayers of people who are not united to Jesus Christ by a living faith in Himself as their Savior and Lord. I do not say that God never answers the prayers of those who are not believers on Jesus Christ. I believe that He sometimes does. He answered some of my prayers before I was, in the Bible sense, a believer on Him, but He does not promise to do it. His doing it belongs to what the old theologians used to call so aptly "the uncovenanted mercies of God." He promises most plainly and most positively to answer the prayers of those who believe on Jesus Christ, but never does He promise to answer the prayers of those who do not believe on Jesus Christ. Anyone who does not believe on Jesus Christ has no right whatsoever to expect God to answer his prayers, and he has no cause whatsoever to complain that the promises of God are not true because He does not answer his prayers. There are many people who say they know that God does not answer prayer because He has never answered their prayers, and they have tried praying time and time again. But that is no proof that God does not answer prayer, for God has never promised to answer their prayers.

ONE OF THE MANY GOOD THINGS ABOUT BELIEVING ON JESUS CHRIST IS THAT IT PUTS US ON PRAYING GROUND; IT PUTS US IN THE PLACE WHERE WE MAY GO TO GOD IN EVERY TIME OF NEED AND GET FROM HIM THE VERY THING THAT WE NEED AND ASK FOR.

One of the many good things about believing on Jesus Christ is that it puts us on praying ground; it puts us in the place where we may go to God in every time of need and get from Him the very thing that we need and ask for. I would rather be on praying ground, rather be in such a relationship to God that He can and will answer my prayers, than to have the combined wealth of a hundred Rockefellers. Times will come in the life of every one of us, sooner or later, when no earthly friend can help us, and no amount of wealth can help us; but the time will never come when God cannot help us and deliver us completely. This important question, therefore, confronts every one of us: "Do I believe on Jesus Christ?" Not do I believe about Him, but do I believe on Him? If you do not, there is but one wise thing to do that has even the slightest semblance of intelligence, and that is to believe on Jesus Christ right now. Put your confidence in Him as your Savior right now, and look to God to forgive your sins right now because Jesus Christ died in your place. Put your confidence in Him right now as your Lord and Master to whom you surrender the entire control of your thoughts and your life and your conduct.

THOSE WHO DO THE LORD'S WILL

But this is not all of the description of those whose prayers God promises to answer. The rest of the description of this fortunate class we find in the verse that follows the promise: *"If you love Me, keep My commandments"* (John 14:15). The promise, therefore, is made to those who believe on Jesus Christ and who love Him with that genuine love that leads them to keep His commandments. Of course, to keep His commandments we must know them, and to know them we must study His Word, in which He has revealed His will to us. Thus we see that the promise is made to those who study the Word of God each day of their lives so that they may know what God's will is regarding their conduct, and who, when they discover it, do it every time. This brings us to just where we were when we were studying 1 John 3:22: *"And whatsoever we ask, we receive of Him, because we keep His commandments, and do those things that are pleasing in His sight."*

There is not a promise in the whole Book of God that God will hear and answer the prayers of a disobedient child. If we are to expect God to listen to us when we pray to Him, we must first of all listen to God when He speaks to us in His Word. We must obey God every time He commands; then, and only then, will He hear us every time we pray. We must study His Word each day of our lives so that we may find out what His will is, and when we find it we must do it every time. Then, and only then, are we on praying ground.

To sum it all up, then, the promise of God to give to a certain class of people whatever they ask in a certain way is made to those who are united to Him by a living faith and an obedient love—to them and to them alone. Someone may ask, "Which is more important in the prayer life, that we have a living faith in Jesus Christ or an obedient love for Jesus Christ?" The answer is simple. You cannot have one without the other. If you have a living faith in Jesus Christ, it will lead inevitably to an obedient love for Jesus Christ. Paul stated this point clearly in Galatians 5:6: "*For in Jesus Christ neither circumcision avails any thing, nor uncircumcision; but faith which works by love.*" On the other hand, you will never love Jesus Christ until you begin by believing in His love for you. We begin by believing in His love for us, and we end by loving Him. Or, as John put it in 1 John 4:19: "*We love Him, because He first loved us.*"

Many people are trying to love God as a matter of duty, but no one ever succeeds in that attempt. Of course, we ought to love God, for He is infinitely worthy of our love. We ought to love Him because of His moral perfection, and because He is the infinite One and our Creator; but no one ever did love Him for these reasons, nor ever will or ever can. Here is where the Unitarians made their mistake. They tried to love God as a matter of duty. We never can and never will. But if we will first of all just put our trust in His wonderful love for us, vile and worthless sinners that we are, we will soon find ourselves loving Him without effort. Love for God is the inevitable outcome of our believing in His love for us.

One day in London, a little girl came to Mark Guy Pearse (1842–1930), the great English preacher, looked up wistfully into his face, and said, "Mr. Pearse, I don't love Jesus. I wish I did love Jesus, but I don't love Jesus. Won't you please tell me how to love Jesus?" And the great preacher looked down into those eager eyes and said to her, "Little girl, as you go home today, keep saying to yourself, 'Jesus loves me. Jesus loves me. Jesus loves me.' And when you come back next Sunday, I think you will be able to say, 'I love Jesus.'"

The following Sunday, the little girl came up to him again. With happy eyes and radiant face she exclaimed, "Oh, Mr. Pearse, I do love Jesus! Last Sunday as I went home I kept saying to myself, 'Jesus loves me. Jesus loves me. Jesus loves me.' I began to think about His love, and I began to think how He died upon the cross in my place, and I found my cold heart growing warm, and the first I knew, it was full of love for Jesus."

That is the only way anyone will ever learn to love the Lord Jesus— by first of all believing what the Bible tells us about His love for us even when we are the vilest of sinners (see Romans 5:8); how He died in our place; how *"He was wounded for our transgressions, He was bruised for our iniquities: the chastisement of our peace was upon Him; and with His stripes we are healed"* (Isaiah 53:5). We begin by believing on Him; we begin by believing in His great love for us, and we wind up loving Him and showing our love to Him by daily studying His Word to find out His will, and doing it every time we find it. Then we are on praying ground.

Some years ago, a great Scottish teacher delivered an address at Northfield on the subject of whether it was better to have faith in Jesus Christ without love, or to have love for Jesus Christ without faith. He came to the conclusion that it was better to have love without faith, than it was to have faith without love. But the whole address, though a great address in many ways, was built upon a misunderstanding and a false assumption. He had assumed that we could have love without faith, but we cannot. Love for Christ is the outcome of faith in Christ, and faith in Christ is the root out of which love for Christ grows. To discuss whether it is better to have faith without love, or love without faith, is like discussing whether it would be better to have an apple orchard whose trees had good roots but bore no apples, or to have an orchard whose trees had no roots but bore good apples. Of course, an orchard where the trees had no roots would bear no apples at all. Likewise, a life that is not rooted in faith in the love of Jesus Christ for us has no roots and cannot bear the fruit of love, and the obedience that comes out of love. So, then, this promise that we are considering is made to those who have a living faith in Jesus Christ that manifests itself in an obedient love.

PRAYING IN THE NAME OF JESUS

But how must those who are united to Jesus Christ by a living faith that reveals itself in an obedient love pray if they are to get the very thing that they ask? Let us read the verse again: *"And whatsoever you shall ask in My name, that will I do, that the Father may be glorified in the Son. If you shall ask any thing in My name, I will do it."* If we are to get from God what we ask, we must ask it in the name of the Lord Jesus. Prayer in the name of Jesus Christ prevails with God. No other prayer does. There is no other approach to God for any man or woman except through Jesus Christ, as the Lord Himself tells us in John 14:6: *"I am the way, the truth, and the life: no man comes to the Father, but by Me."*

But just what does it mean to pray in the name of Jesus? I have heard many explanations of this. Some of them were so profound, so mysterious, so mixed, or so obscure that when I finished reading them or listening to them, I knew less about it than when I started. I have heard two great Bible teachers, two of the most renowned Bible teachers in the world, say that to "pray in the name of Jesus means to pray in the person of Jesus." Now I do not question that these two Bible teachers had some definite thought in their own minds, but it certainly conveyed no clear and definite thought to my mind. The truth is, there is nothing mysterious about this matter. It is as simple as anything possibly can be, so simple that any intelligent child can understand it.

I am always suspicious of profound explanations of the Scriptures, explanations that require a scholar or philosopher to understand them. The Bible is the plain man's Book. The Lord Jesus Himself said in Matthew 11:25, *"I thank You, O Father, Lord of heaven and earth, because You have hidden these things from the wise and prudent, and have revealed them to babes."* In at least ninety-nine cases in a hundred, the meaning of Scripture that lies on the surface, the meaning that any simple-minded man, woman, or child who really wants to know the truth and to obey it would see in it, is what it really means.

I have great sympathy with the little child who, when she once heard an educated attempt to explain away the plain meaning of Scripture, exclaimed, "If God did not mean what He said, why didn't He say what He meant?" Well, God always does say just what He means, just what you and I would understand by it if our wills were really surrendered to God, if we really desired to know exactly what God wished to tell us and not to read our own opinions into the Bible. By this expression, "*in My name*," He means exactly what the words would indicate to any earnest and intelligent seeker of the truth who was willing to take God's words at their exact face value.

When you come across a word or a phrase in the Bible and do not know what it means, the thing to do is not to run off to a dictionary, a commentary, or some book of theology, but to take your concordance, go through the Bible, and look up every place where that word or phrase, or synonymous words or phrases, are used. Then you will know just what the word or phrase means. The meaning of words and phrases in the Bible is to be determined just as it is in all other books—by usage. I have done this with the phrase "*in My name*" and with the synonymous phrases "*in His name*" and "*in the name of Jesus Christ*." I have looked up every passage in the Bible where they are found, and I have discovered what I suspected at the outset—that these phrases mean exactly the same in the Bible as they do in ordinary, everyday speech.

What does it mean in ordinary, everyday speech to ask something in another person's name? Let me illustrate what it means. Suppose I were to walk into a bank at which I do not have an account. I write out a check, "Pay to the order of R. A. Torrey the sum of five dollars." Then I sign my own name at the bottom of the check, go to the teller's window, and ask to cash that check. What would I be doing? I would be asking that bank to give me five dollars. And in whose name would I be asking it? In my own name. And what would happen? The teller would take the check and look at it, and then look at me, and then he would say, "Dr. Torrey, do you have an account at this bank?"

"No."

Then what would the teller say? Something like this: "We would like to accommodate you, but that is not good business. You have no claim whatsoever on this bank, and we cannot honor your check even though it is for only five dollars." But suppose, instead of that, some man who had a hundred thousand dollars in that bank were to call me and say, "Dr. Torrey, I am greatly interested in the work of the Bible Institute. I have wanted to give some money toward it, and I am going to hand it to you." And then he makes out a check, "Pay to the order of R. A. Torrey the sum of five thousand dollars," and signs his name at the bottom of the check. So I go to the bank again. In presenting that check, what would I be doing? I would be asking that bank to give me five thousand dollars. And in whose name would I be asking it? Not in my own name, but in the name of the man whose name is signed at the bottom of the check, and who has claims of a hundred thousand dollars on that bank.

What would happen? The teller would look at the check, and he would not ask me whether I had any money in that bank. He would not care whether I had a penny in that bank or in any bank. If the check were properly written, and properly endorsed, he would count me out five thousand dollars; for I would be asking it in the other man's name, asking it on the ground of his claims on that bank.

Now that is exactly what praying in the name of Jesus Christ means. It means that we go to the Bank of Heaven, on which neither you nor I nor any other man on earth has any claim of his own, but upon which Jesus Christ has infinite claims. In Jesus's name, which He has given us a right to put on our checks, if we are united to Him by a living faith that reveals itself in an obedient love, we may ask whatever we need. Or, to put it another way, to pray in the name of Jesus Christ is to recognize that we have no claims on God whatsoever, that God owes us nothing whatsoever, that we deserve nothing from God; but, believing what God Himself tells us about Jesus Christ's claims upon Him, we ask God for things on the grounds of Jesus Christ's claims upon God. And when we draw near to God in that way, we can get *whatever we ask*, no matter how great it may be.

Praying in the name of Christ means more than merely attaching the phrase "in Jesus's name" or "for Jesus's sake" to your prayers. Many people ask for things and attach those phrases to their prayers, while all the while they are really approaching God on the ground of some claim that they only imagine they have on God. In reality, though they use the phrase, they are not praying in the name of Jesus Christ but praying in their own name. A man who realizes that he has no claims on God might not put that phrase in his prayer at all, but he can believe that Jesus Christ has claims on God and can approach God on the grounds of Jesus Christ's claims.

Here is where many people fail in getting an answer to prayer. Such people may ask things of God on the grounds of some claim they imagine they have on God. They think that because they are such good Christians, so consistent in their lives and so active in their service, God is under obligation to grant their prayers.

In Melbourne, Australia, as I went on the platform one day at a businessmen's meeting, a note was put in my hands. This note read as follows:

Dear Dr. Torrey:

I am in great perplexity. I have been praying for a long time for something that I am confident is according to God's will, but I do not get it. I have been a member of the Presbyterian Church for thirty years, and have tried to be a consistent one all the time. I have been superintendent in the Sunday school for twenty-five years, and an elder in the church for twenty years; and yet God does not answer my prayer, and I cannot understand it. Can you explain it to me?

I took the note with me on to the platform and read it and said, "It is perfectly easy to explain. This man thinks that because he has been a

consistent church member for thirty years, a faithful Sunday school superintendent for twenty-five years, and an elder in the church for twenty
years, God is under obligation to answer his prayer. He is really praying
in his own name, and God will not hear our prayers when we approach
Him in that way. We must, if we want God to answer our prayers, give
up any thought that we have any claims on God. Not one of us deserves
anything from God. If we got what we deserved, every last one of us
would spend eternity in hell. But Jesus Christ has great claims on God,
and we should go to God in our prayers, not on the grounds of any
goodness in ourselves, but on the grounds of Jesus Christ's claims."

At the close of the meeting, a gentleman stepped up to me and said,
"I wrote that note. You have hit the nail square on the head. I did think
that because I had been a consistent church member for thirty years,
a Sunday school superintendent for twenty-five years, and an elder in
the church for twenty years, God was under obligation to answer my
prayers. I see my mistake."

Multitudes are making the same mistake. They imagine that because they are faithful church members, and active in Christian service,
God is under obligation to answer their prayers, and they have some
claim on God. Not one of us has any claim on God. We are all miserable
sinners. But Jesus Christ has claims on God, and He has given us the
right to draw near to God in His name, that is, on the grounds of His
claims on God.

NOT ONE OF US HAS ANY CLAIM ON GOD. WE
ARE ALL MISERABLE SINNERS. BUT JESUS
CHRIST HAS CLAIMS ON GOD, AND HE HAS
GIVEN US THE RIGHT TO DRAW NEAR TO GOD
IN HIS NAME, THAT IS, ON THE GROUNDS OF
HIS CLAIMS ON GOD.

Therefore, to pray in the name of Jesus Christ means simply this: that we recognize that we have no claims whatsoever on God; that we have no merit whatsoever in His sight; and furthermore, that Jesus Christ has immeasurable claims on God, and has given us the right to draw near to God, not on the grounds of our claims, but on the grounds of His claims. When we thus draw near to God in prayer, God will give us what we ask.

What a precious privilege it is to pray in the name of Jesus Christ! How rich we are if we only realize that Jesus Christ has given us the privilege of drawing near to the heavenly Father in His name, on the grounds of His claims on God. When I was a boy, my father had put my brother next older than me in charge of the expenditures of the home, because my oldest brother was away from home. The bank account was in the name of this brother next older than me. But he, too, was called away from home, and so he turned over to me the matter of paying bills and the conduct of the business. He gave me a checkbook full of blank checks with his signature on them and said, "Whenever you want any money, just fill out one of these checks for the amount that you want, and go and present it at the bank."

How rich I felt with that checkbook full of blank checks! I could fill one out at any time and go to the bank and get what I asked for. But what is that compared with what the Lord Jesus Christ has done for us? He has put His entire bank account at our disposal. He has given us the right to draw near to the Father in His name, and to ask anything of God on the grounds not of our claims on God, but on the grounds of His claims on God.

Even before D. L. Moody gave up business, he was active in Christian work and often went out from Chicago to some of the country towns and held short series of meetings. At one time he was holding a series of meetings in a town in Illinois some distance from Chicago. The wife of the judge of that district came to him and said, "Mr. Moody, won't you go and talk to my husband?"

Mr. Moody replied, "I cannot talk to your husband. Your husband is an educated man; I am nothing but an ignorant shoe clerk from Chicago."

But the judge's wife was very insistent that he should go and talk with him, and finally Mr. Moody consented to go. When he entered the outer office of the judge, the law clerks snickered audibly as they thought of how quickly the clever judge would dispose of this ignorant young worker from Chicago. Mr. Moody went into the judge's inner office and said to him, "Judge, I cannot talk with you. You are an educated man, and I am nothing but an uneducated shoe salesman from Chicago. But I want to ask you one thing. When you are converted, will you let me know?"

The judge answered with a contemptuous laugh, "Yes, young man, when I am converted I will let you know. Yes, when I am converted I will let you know. Good day."

As Mr. Moody passed out of the inner office to the outer office, the judge raised his voice higher so that the clerks in the outer office might hear, "Yes, young man, when I am converted I will let you know," and the law clerks snickered louder than before.

But the judge was converted within a year. Mr. Moody went back to the town and called on the judge. He said, "Judge, do you mind telling me how you were converted?"

"No, Mr. Moody," he replied, "I will be very glad to tell you. One night after you were here, my wife went to the prayer meeting as she always did, and I stayed home as I always did and read the evening paper. After a while, as I sat there reading, I began to feel very miserable. I began to feel that I was a great sinner. Before my wife got home, I was so miserable that I did not dare face my wife, and I went to bed before she reached the house. She came up to my room and asked, 'Are you ill?' I replied, 'No, I wasn't feeling well and thought I would go to bed. Good night.' I was miserable all night, and when morning came I felt so bad that I did not dare face my wife at the breakfast table. I simply looked into the breakfast room and said, 'Wife, I am not feeling well. I'll not eat any breakfast this morning. Good-bye, I am going down to the office.' When I got to the office, I felt so miserable that I told my clerks that they could take a holiday. When they had left, I locked the outer door, went into my inner office, locked that door, and sat down. I felt more and more miserable as I thought of my sins, until at last I knelt down and said, 'Oh, God, forgive my sins.' There was no answer. And I cried more earnestly, 'Oh, God, forgive my sins.' There was still no answer. I would not say, 'Oh, God, for Jesus Christ's sake forgive my sins,' for I was a Unitarian and did not believe in the atonement. Again I cried, 'Oh, God, forgive my sins.' But there was no answer. At last I was so perfectly miserable at the thought of my sins that I cried, 'Oh, God, for Jesus Christ's sake forgive my sins.' And I found instant peace."

There is no use in our trying to approach God in any other way than in the name of Jesus Christ, on the grounds of His claims upon God, and on the grounds of His atoning death, by which He took our sins upon Himself and made it possible for us to approach God on the grounds of His claims upon God.

While we have no claims upon God because of any goodness or service of our own, Jesus Christ, as I have said, has infinite claims upon God and has given us the right to approach God in His name. Thus, we ought to go boldly to God and ask great things of God. Oftentimes, when we pray and ask something that seems to be pretty big, the devil will come and say to us, "You ought not to pray for anything so great as that. You are such a poor Christian, and that is more than you deserve." Yes, it is more than we deserve, but it is not as much as Jesus Christ deserves. Time and again Satan has said to me when I have dared to ask something of God that seemed very large, "Oh, don't dare to ask as great a thing as that. You are not worthy of anything as great as that." I have replied, "I know that I am not worthy of anything as great as that. I am not worthy of anything at all, but Jesus Christ is worthy of that, and I am asking not on the ground of my claims upon God, but on the grounds of His." Sometimes, as I think of how precious the name of Jesus Christ is to God, how He delights to honor the name of His Son, I grow very bold and ask God for great things.

Do you realize that we honor the name of Christ by asking great things in His name? Do you realize that we dishonor that name by not daring to ask great things in His name? Oh, have faith in the power of Jesus's name, and dare to ask great things in His name!

During the Civil War, there was a father and mother in Columbus, Ohio, who had an only son, the joy of their hearts. Soon after the outbreak of the war, he came home one day and said to his father and mother, "I have enlisted in the army." Of course, they felt badly to have their son leave home, but they loved their country and were willing to make the sacrifice of giving their son to go to the war and fight for his country. After he had gone to the front, he wrote home regularly, telling his father and mother about his experiences in camp and elsewhere. His letters were full of brightness and good cheer, and they brought joy to the father's and mother's lonely hearts. But one day at the regular time, no letter came.

Days passed, and no letter. Weeks passed, and they wondered what might have happened to their boy. One day a letter came from the United States government, and in it they were told that there had been a great battle, that many had been killed, and that their son was among those who had been killed in battle. The light went out of that home. Days and weeks, months and years passed by. The war came to an end. One morning as they were sitting at the breakfast table, the maid came in and said, "There is a poor, ragged fellow at the door, and he wants to speak to you. But I knew you did not wish to speak to a man like him, and he handed me this note and asked me to put it in your hand." And she put in the hands of the father a soiled and crumpled piece of paper. The father opened it, and when he glanced at it his eyes fell upon the writing. Then he was startled, for he recognized the writing of his son. The note said:

Dear Father and Mother:

I have been shot and have only a short time to live, and I am writing you this last farewell note. As I write, there is kneeling beside me my most intimate friend in the company, and when the war is over he will bring you this note. When he does, be kind to him for Charlie's sake.

Your son, Charles

There was nothing in that house that was too good for that poor tramp "for Charlie's sake," and there is nothing in heaven or on earth too good, or too great, for you and me in Jesus's name. Oh, be bold and ask great things of God in Jesus's name!

18

HINTS FOR THE
INNER CHAMBER

Andrew Murray

At the conference there was a brother who had earnestly confessed his neglect of prayer, but who was able, later, to declare that his eyes had been opened to see that the Lord really supplied grace for all that He required from us. In sincerity he asked if some hints could not be given as to the best way of spending time profitably in the inner chamber. There was no opportunity then for giving an answer. Perhaps the following thoughts may be of help.

1. As you enter the inner chamber, let your first work be to thank God for the unspeakable love that invites you to come to Him and to converse freely with Him.

If your heart is cold and dead, remember that religion is not a matter of feeling but has to do first with the will. Raise your heart to God and thank Him for the assurance you have that He looks down on you and will bless you. Through such an act of faith you honor God and draw your soul away from being occupied with itself. Think also of the glorious grace of the Lord Jesus, who is willing to teach you to pray and to give you the disposition to do so. Think, too, of the Holy Spirit who was purposely given to cry, *"Abba, Father"* (Galatians 4:6), in your heart and to help your weakness in prayer. Five minutes spent thus will strengthen your faith for your work in the inner chamber. Once more I say, begin with an act of thanksgiving and praise God for the inner chamber and the promise of blessing there.

2. *You must prepare yourself for prayer by prayerful Bible study.*

The great reason why the inner chamber is not attractive is that people do not know how to pray. Their stock of words is soon exhausted, and they do not know what to say further. This happens because they forget that prayer is not a soliloquy, where everything comes from one side, but it is a dialogue, where God's child listens to what the Father says, replies to it, and then asks for the things he needs.

Read a few verses from the Bible. Do not concern yourself with the difficulties contained in them. You can consider these later; but take what you understand, apply it to yourself, and ask the Father to make His Word light and power in your heart. Thus you will have material enough for prayer from the Word that the Father speaks to you; you will also have the liberty to ask for things you need. Keep on in this way, and the inner chamber will become at length, not a place where you sigh and struggle only, but one of living fellowship with the Father in heaven. Prayerful study of the Bible is indispensable for powerful prayer.

3. *When you have thus received the Word into your heart, turn to prayer.*

But do not attempt it hastily or thoughtlessly, as though you knew well enough how to pray. Prayer in our own strength brings no blessing. Take time to present yourself reverently and in quietness before God. Remember His greatness and holiness and love. Think over what you wish to ask from Him. Do not be satisfied with going over the same things every day. No child goes on saying the same thing day after day to his earthly father.

Conversation with the Father is colored by the needs of the day. Let your prayers be something definite, arising either out of the Word that you have read, or out of the real soul needs that you long to have satisfied. Let your prayers be so definite that you can say as you go out, "I know what I have asked from my Father, and I expect an answer."

It is a good plan sometimes to take a piece of paper and write down what you wish to pray for. You might keep such a paper for a week or more and repeat the prayers until some new need arises.

4. We are allowed to pray that we may help also in the needs of others.

What has been said is in reference your own needs. One great reason why prayer in the inner chamber does not bring more joy and blessing is that it is too selfish, and selfishness is the death of prayer.

Remember your family, your congregation, with its interests, your own neighborhood, and the church to which you belong. Let your heart be enlarged and take up the interests of missions and of the church throughout the whole world. Become an intercessor, and you will experience for the first time the blessedness of prayer, as you find out that God will make use of you to share His blessing with others through prayer. You will begin to feel that there is something worth living for, as you find that you have something to say to God, and that from heaven He will do things in answer to your prayers that otherwise would not have been done.

A child can ask his father for bread. A full-grown son converses with him about all the interests of his business and about his further purposes. A weak child of God prays only for himself, but a full-grown man in Christ understands how to consult with God over what must take place in the kingdom. Let your prayer list bear the names of those for whom you pray: your minister, and all other ministers, and the different missionary affairs with which you are connected. Thus the inner chamber will really become a wonder of God's goodness and a fountain of great joy. It will become the most blessed place on earth. It is a great thing to say, but it is the simple truth, that God will make it a Bethel, where His angels will ascend and descend, and where you will cry out,

"Then shall the Lord *be my God"* (Genesis 28:21). He will make it also Peniel, where you will see the face of God, as a prince of God, as one who wrestled with the angel and overcame him. (See Genesis 32:30.)

5. Do not forget the close bond between the inner chamber and the outer world.

The attitude of the inner chamber must remain with us all the day. The object of the inner chamber is to so unite us with God that we may have Him always abiding with us. Sin, thoughtlessness, and yielding to the flesh or to the world make us unfit for the inner chamber and bring a cloud over the soul. If you have stumbled or fallen, return to the inner chamber; let your first work be to invoke the blood of Jesus and to claim cleansing by it. Do not rest until by confession you have repented of and put away your sin. Let the precious blood really give you a fresh freedom of approach to God. Remember that the roots of your life in the inner chamber strike far out in body and soul so as to manifest themselves in business life. Let the *"obedience of faith"* (Romans 16:26), in which you pray in secret, rule you constantly. The inner chamber is intended to bind man to God, to supply him with power from God, to enable him to live for God alone. Let God be thanked for the inner chamber and for the blessed life that He will enable us to experience and nourish there.

TIME

Before the creation of the world, time did not exist. God lived in eternity in a way that we little understand. With creation, time began, and everything was placed under its power. God has placed all living creatures under a law of slow growth. Think of the length of time it takes for a child to become a man in body and mind. In learning, in wisdom, in business, in handicraft, and in politics, everything somehow depends on patience and perseverance. Everything needs time.

It is just the same in religion. There can be no communion with a holy God, no fellowship between heaven and earth, no power for the salvation of the souls of others, unless much time is set apart for it. Just as it is necessary for a child, for long years, to eat and learn every day, so the life of grace depends entirely on the time men are willing to give to it day by day.

The minister is appointed by God to teach and help those who are engaged in the ordinary avocations of life to find time and to use it properly for the preservation of the spiritual life. The minister cannot do this unless he himself has a living experience of a life of prayer. His highest calling is not preaching, or speaking, or parochial visitation, but it is to cultivate the life of God daily and to be a witness of what the Lord teaches him and accomplishes in him.

Was it not so with the Lord Jesus? Why did He, who had no sin to confess, sometimes have to spend all night in prayer to God? Because the divine life had to be strengthened in communication with His Father. His experience of a life in which He took time for fellowship with God has enabled Him to share that life with us.

Oh, that each minister might understand that he has received his time from God so that he might serve Him with it! God must have the first and the best of your time for fellowship with Himself. Without this, your preaching and labor have little power. Here on earth I may spend my time for the money or the learning which I receive in exchange. The minister can exchange his time for the divine power and the spiritual blessings to be obtained from heaven. That, and nothing else, makes him a man of God and ensures that his preaching will be in the demonstration of the Spirit and power.

19

ANSWERS TO PRAYER

E. M. Bounds

In his *Soldier's Pocket Book*, Lord Wolseley says that if a young officer wishes to succeed, he must volunteer for the most hazardous duties and take every possible chance of risking his life. It was a spirit and courage like that which was shown in the service of God by a good soldier of Jesus Christ named John McKenzie. One evening when he was a lad and eager for work in the foreign mission field he knelt down at the foot of a tree and offered up this prayer: "O Lord send me to the darkest spot on earth." And God heard him and sent him to South Africa where he labored many years first under the London Missionary Society and then under the British Government as the first Resident Commissioner among the natives of Bechuanaland.

—J. O. Struthers

Answered prayer brings praying out of the realm of dry, dead things and makes praying a thing of life and power. It is the answer to prayer that brings things to pass, changes the natural trend of things, and orders all things according to the will of God. It is the answer to prayer that takes praying out of the regions of fanaticism and saves it from being utopian, or from being merely fanciful. It is the answer to prayer that makes praying a power for God and for man, and makes praying real and divine. Unanswered prayers are training schools for unbelief, an imposition and a nuisance, an impertinence to God and to man.

Answers to prayer are the only surety that we have prayed aright. What marvelous power there is in prayer! What untold miracles it works in this world! What untold benefits to men does it secure to those who pray! Why is it that the average prayer goes begging for an answer?

The millions of unanswered prayers are not to be solved by the mystery of God's will. We are not the sport of His sovereign power. He is not playing at make-believe in His marvelous promises to answer prayer. The whole explanation is found in our wrong praying. We ask and do not receive because we *"ask amiss"* (James 4:3). If all unanswered prayers were dumped into the ocean, they would come very near filling it.

Child of God, can you pray? Are your prayers answered? If not, why not? Answered prayer is the proof of your real praying.

The efficacy of prayer from a Bible standpoint lies solely in the answer to prayer. The benefit of prayer has been well and popularly maximized by the saying, "It moves the arm that moves the universe."

To get unquestioned answers to prayer is not only important as to the satisfying of our desires, but it is the evidence of our abiding in Christ. Thus, it becomes more important still. The mere act of praying is no test of our relationship to God. The act of praying may be a dead performance. It may be the routine of habit. But to pray and receive clear answers, not once or twice, but daily, is the sure test and is the gracious point of our vital connection with Jesus Christ. Read our Lord's words in this connection: *"If you abide in Me, and My words abide in you, you shall ask what you will, and it shall be done to you"* (John 15:7).

To God and to man, the answer to prayer is the all-important part of our praying. The answer to prayer, direct and unmistakable, is the evidence of God's existence. It proves that God lives, that there is a God, an intelligent Being, who is interested in His creatures, and who listens to them when they approach Him in prayer. There is no proof so clear and demonstrative that God exists than prayer and its answer. This was Elijah's plea: *"Hear me, O LORD, hear me, that this people may know that You are the LORD God"* (1 Kings 18:37).

The answer to prayer is the part of prayer that glorifies God. Unanswered prayers are dumb oracles that leave the praying ones in darkness, doubt, and bewilderment, and that carry no conviction to the unbeliever. It is not the act or the attitude of praying that gives efficacy to prayer. It is not abject prostration of the body before God, the vehement or quiet utterance to God, or the exquisite beauty and poetry of the diction of our prayers that do the deed. It is not the marvelous array of argument and eloquence in praying that makes prayer effectual. Not one or all of these are the things that glorify God. It is the answer that brings glory to His name.

Elijah might have prayed on Carmel's heights until this day, with all the fire and energy of his soul, but if no answer had been given, no glory would have come to God. Peter might have shut himself up with Dorcas' dead body until he himself died on his knees, but if no answer had come, no glory to God nor good to man would have followed. Only doubt, blight, and dismay would be the result.

Answer to prayer is the convincing proof of our right relations to God. Jesus said at the grave of Lazarus:

> *Father, I thank You that You have heard Me. And I knew that You hear Me always: but because of the people which stand by I said it, that they may believe that You have sent Me.* (John 11:41–42)

The answer to His prayer was the proof of His mission from God, just as the answer to Elijah's prayer was made to the woman whose son he raised to life. She said, *"Now by this I know that you are a man of God"*

(1 Kings 17:24). He is highest in the favor of God who has the readiest access and the greatest number of answers to prayer from Almighty God.

Prayer ascends to God by an invariable law, even by more than law—by the will, the promise, and the presence of a personal God. The answer comes back to earth by all the promise, the truth, the power, and the love of God. Not to be concerned about the answer to prayer is not to pray. What a world of waste there is in praying! What myriads of prayers have been offered for which no answer is returned, no answer is longed for, and no answer is expected!

We have been nurturing a false faith and hiding the shame of our loss and inability to pray by the false, comforting plea that God does not answer directly or objectively, but indirectly and subjectively. We have persuaded ourselves that by some kind of hocus-pocus, of which we are wholly unconscious about its process and its results, we have been made better.

Fully aware that God has not answered us directly, we have solaced ourselves with the delusive balm that God has in some impalpable way, and with unknown results, given us something better. Or we have comforted and nurtured our spiritual sloth by saying that it is not God's will to give it to us.

Faith teaches God's praying ones that it is God's will to answer prayer. God answers all prayers and every prayer of His children who truly pray.

Prayer makes darkened clouds withdraw,
Prayer climbs the ladder Jacob saw;
Gives exercise to faith and love,
Brings every blessing from above.

The emphasis in the Scriptures is always given to the answer to prayer. All things from God are given in answer to prayer. God Himself, His presence, His gifts, and His grace, one and all, are secured by prayer. The medium by which God communicates with men is prayer. The most real thing in prayer, its very essential end, is the answer it secures. The mere repetition of words in prayer, the counting of beads, the multiplying of mere words as works of uncalled-for obligation—as if there were virtue in the number of prayers to avail—is a vain delusion, an empty thing, a useless service. Prayer looks directly to securing an answer. This is its design. It has no other end in view.

ALL THINGS FROM GOD ARE GIVEN IN ANSWER TO PRAYER. GOD HIMSELF, HIS PRESENCE, HIS GIFTS, AND HIS GRACE, ONE AND ALL, ARE SECURED BY PRAYER. THE MEDIUM BY WHICH GOD COMMUNICATES WITH MEN IS PRAYER. THE MOST REAL THING IN PRAYER, ITS VERY ESSENTIAL END, IS THE ANSWER IT SECURES.

Communion with God, of course, is in prayer. There is sweet fellowship with our God through His Holy Spirit. Enjoyment of God is in praying—sweet, rich, and strong. The graces of the Spirit in the inner soul are nurtured by prayer, kept alive and promoted in their growth by this spiritual exercise. But not one or even all these benefits of prayer have in them the essential end of prayer. The divinely appointed channel through which all good and all grace flows to our souls and bodies is prayer.

Prayer is appointed to convey
The blessings God designs to give.

Prayer is divinely ordained as the means by which all temporal and spiritual good are directed to us. Prayer is not an end in itself. It is not something done to be rested in, not something we have done, about which we are to congratulate ourselves. It is a means to an end. It is something we do that brings us something in return, without which the praying is valueless. Prayer always aims at securing an answer.

We are rich and strong, good and holy, generous and kind by answered prayer. It is not the mere performance, the attitude, or the words of prayer that bring benefit to us, but it is the answer sent directly from heaven. Conscious, real answers to prayer bring real good to us. This is not praying merely for self or simply for selfish ends. The selfish character cannot exist when the prayer conditions are fulfilled.

It is by these answered prayers that human nature is enriched. The answered prayer brings us into constant, conscious communion with God, awakens and enlarges gratitude, and excites the melody and lofty inspiration of praise. Answered prayer is the mark of God in our praying. It is the exchange with heaven, and it establishes and realizes a relationship with the unseen. We give our prayers in exchange for the divine blessing. God accepts our prayers through the atoning blood and gives Himself, His presence, and His grace in return.

All holy attitudes are affected by answered prayers. By the answers to prayer all holy principles are matured, and faith, love, and hope have their enrichment by answered prayer. The answer is found in all true praying. The answer is strongly in prayer as an aim, a desire expressed; its expectation and realization give importunity and realization to prayer. It is the fact of the answer that makes the prayer and that enters into its very being.

To seek no answer to prayer takes the desire, the aim, and the heart out of prayer. It makes praying a dead, foolish thing, fit only for dumb idols. It is the answer that brings praying into biblical regions and makes it a desire realized, a pursuit, an interest. The answer clothes it with flesh and blood and makes it a prayer, throbbing with all the true life of prayer, affluent with all the paternal relations of giving and receiving, of asking and answering.

God holds all good in His own hands. That good comes to us through our Lord Jesus Christ, only because of His atoning merits, by asking it in His name. The only and the sole command in which all the others of its class belong, is: *"Ask...seek...knock"* (Matthew 7:7). And the promise is its counterpart, its necessary equivalent, and its result: *"It shall be given you...you shall find...it shall be opened to you"* (verse 7). God is so much involved in prayer and its hearing and answering that all His attributes and His whole being are centered in that great fact. It distinguishes Him as particularly beneficent, wonderfully good, and powerfully attractive in His nature. *"O You that hears prayer, to You shall all flesh come"* (Psalm 65:2).

Faithful, O Lord, Thy mercies are,
A rock that cannot move;
A thousand promises declare
Thy constancy of love.

Not only does the Word of God stand as assurance for the answer to prayer, but all the attributes of God conspire to the same end. God's veracity is at stake in the engagements to answer prayer. His wisdom, His truthfulness, and His goodness are involved. God's infinite and inflexible righteousness is pledged to the great end of answering the prayers of those who call upon Him in time of need. Justice and mercy blend into oneness to secure the answer to prayer. It is significant that the very justice of God comes into play and stands hard by God's faithfulness in the strong promise God makes of the pardon of sins and of cleansing from sin's pollution. *"If we confess our sins, He is faithful and just to forgive us our sins, and to cleanse us from all unrighteousness"* (1 John 1:9).

God's kingly relation to man, with all its authority, unites with the fatherly relationship and with all its tenderness, to secure the answer to prayer.

Our Lord Jesus Christ is most fully committed to the answer of prayer. *"And whatsoever you shall ask in My name, that will I do, that the Father may be glorified in the Son"* (John 14:13). How well assured the answer to prayer is, when that answer is to glorify God the Father! And how eager Jesus Christ is to glorify His Father in heaven! So eager is He to answer prayer that always and everywhere brings glory to the Father, that no prayer offered in His name is denied or overlooked by Him. Says our Lord Jesus Christ again, giving fresh assurance to our faith, *"If you shall ask any thing in My name, I will do it"* (verse 14). So says He once more, *"Ask what you will, and it shall be done to you"* (John 15:7).

> Come, my soul, thy suit prepare,
> Jesus loves to answer prayer;
> He Himself has bid thee pray,
> Therefore will not say thee nay.

20

BOLDNESS AT THE THRONE OF GRACE

Charles Spurgeon

O God! We do not want to speak to You as from a distance, or stand like trembling Israel under the law at a distance from the burning mount. We have not come to Mount Sinai, but to Mount Zion, and that is a place for holy joy and thankfulness, not for terror and bondage. Blessed be Your name, O Lord! We have learned to call You *"Our Father which is in heaven"* (Matthew 6:9). There is reverence, for You are in heaven. But there is sweet familiarity, for You are our Father.

We want to draw very near to You now through Jesus Christ the mediator, and we want to be bold to speak to You as a man speaks with his friend. Have You not said by Your Spirit, *"Let us therefore come boldly to the throne of grace"* (Hebrews 4:16)? We might well flee from Your face if we only remembered our sinfulness. Lord, we do remember it with shame and sorrow. We are grieved to think we have offended You and have neglected Your sweet love and tender mercy so long. But we have *"now returned to the Shepherd and Bishop of* [our] *souls"* (1 Peter 2:25). Led by such grace, we look to Him whom we crucified. We have mourned for Him and then have mourned for our sin.

Now, Lord, we confess our guilt before You with tenderness of heart. We pray that You would seal home to every believer that full and free, that perfect and irreversible charter of forgiveness that You gave to all who put their trust in Jesus Christ. Lord, You have said, *"If we confess our sins,* [You are] *faithful and just to forgive us our sins, and to cleanse us from all unrighteousness"* (1 John 1:9). There is the sin confessed. There is the ransom accepted. Therefore, we know we have peace with God, and we bless that glorious One who has come *"to finish the transgression, and to make an end of sins, and...to bring in everlasting righteousness"* (Daniel 9:24), which, by faith, we take unto ourselves and You impute unto us.

Now, Lord, will You be pleased to cause all Your children's hearts to dance within them for joy? Oh, help Your people to come to Jesus again today. May we be looking unto Him now as we did at first. May we never take our eyes away from His divine person, from His infinite merit, from His finished work, from His living power, or from the expectancy of His speedy coming to *"judge the world with righteousness, and the people with His truth"* (Psalm 96:13).

Bless all Your people with some special gift. If we might make a choice of one, it would be this: *"Quicken* [us] *according to Your word"* (Psalm 119:25). We have life. Give it to us more abundantly. Oh, that we might have so much life that out of the midst of us there might *"flow rivers of living water"* (John 7:38). Lord, make us useful. Dear Savior, use the very least among us. Take the one talent and let it be invested for interest for the great Father. May it please You to show each one of us what You would have us to do. In our families, in our businesses, in the walks of ordinary life, may we be serving the Lord. May we often speak a word for His name and help in some way to scatter the light among the ever growing darkness. Before we go to be with You, may we have sown some seed that we will bring with us on our shoulders in the form of sheaves of blessing.

Lord God, bless our Sunday schools, and give a greater interest in such work, so that there may be no lack of men and women who are glad and happy in teaching the young. Impress this, we pray, upon Your people just now. Move men who have gifts and ability to preach the gospel. There are many who live in villages, and there is no preaching of the gospel near them. Lord, set them to preaching themselves. May You move some hearts so powerfully that their tongues cannot be quiet any longer, and may they attempt in some way, either personally or by supporting someone, to bring the gospel into dark, benighted hamlets so that the people may know the truth.

O Lord, stir up the dwellers in this great, great city. Arouse us to the spiritual destitution of the masses. O God, help us all by some means, by any means, by every means, to get at the ears of men for Christ's sake so that we may reach their hearts. We send up an exceedingly great and sorrowful cry to You on behalf of the millions who enter no place of worship, but rather violate its sanctity and despise its blessed message. Lord, wake up London, we implore You. Send us another Jonah. Send us another John the Baptist. Oh, that Christ Himself would send forth multitudes of laborers among this thick-standing corn, for *the harvest truly is plenteous, but the laborers are few*" (Matthew 9:37). O God! Save this city; save this country; save all countries, and let Your kingdom come. May every knee bow, and may all confess that Jesus Christ is Lord. (See Philippians 2:10–11.)

Our most earnest prayers go up to heaven to You now for great sinners, for men and women who are polluted and depraved by the filthiest of sins. With sovereign mercy make a raid among them. Come and capture some of these so that they may become great lovers of Him who forgives them, and may they become great champions for the cross.

Lord, look upon the multitudes of rich people in this city who know nothing about the gospel and do not wish to know. Oh, that somehow the spiritually poor might be rich with the gospel of Jesus Christ. And then, Lord, look upon the multitude of the poor and the working classes who think religion is a perfectly unnecessary thing for them. By some means, we pray, get them to think and bring them to listen, for "*faith comes by hearing, and hearing by the word of God*" (Romans 10:17).

Above all, O Holy Spirit, descend more mightily. O God, flood the land until there are streams of righteousness. Is there not a promise that says, "*I will pour water upon him that is thirsty, and floods upon the dry ground*" (Isaiah 44:3)? Lord, set Your people praying. Stir up the church to greater prayerfulness.

Now, as You have told us to do, we pray for the people among whom we dwell. We pray for those in authority in the land, asking every blessing for those in government; Your guidance and direction for the Parliament; and Your blessing to all judges and rulers and also upon the poorest of the poor and the lowest of the low. Lord, bless the people. "*Let the people praise You, O God; let all the people praise You*" (Psalm 67:3), for Jesus Christ's sake. Amen.

21

THANKSGIVING

D. L. Moody

The next element of prayer I want to discuss is thanksgiving. We ought to be more thankful for what we receive from God. Perhaps some of you who are mothers have a child in your family who is constantly complaining, never thankful. You know that there is not much pleasure in doing anything for a child like that. If you meet a beggar who is always grumbling and never seems to be thankful for what you give, you very soon shut the door in his face altogether. Ingratitude is about the hardest thing we have to deal with. Shakespeare wrote,

Blow, blow, thou winter wind,
Thou art not so unkind
As man's ingratitude;
Thy tooth is not so keen,
Because thou art not seen,
Although thy breath be rude.

We cannot speak too plainly of this evil, which so demeans those who are guilty of it. Even in Christians there is too much ingratitude! Here we are, getting blessings from God day after day, yet how little praise and thanksgiving there is in the church of God!

William Gurnall, in his *The Christian in Complete Armour*, referring to the words, *"In every thing give thanks"* (1 Thessalonians 5:18), said,

> *"Praise is comely for the upright."* [Psalm 33:1] ...An unthankful saint carries a contradiction with it. "Evil" and "unthankful" are the twins that live and die together. As any ceaseth to be evil, he begins to be thankful.
>
> Consider it is that which God both expects and promiseth himself at your hands; he made you for this end. When the vote passed in heaven for your being, yea happy being, in Christ, it was upon this account, that you should be "a name and a praise" to him on earth in time and in heaven to eternity. Should God miss of this, he would fail of one main part of his design. What prompts him to bestow every mercy, but to afford you matter to compose a song for his praise? They are "a people, children that will not lie: so he became their Saviour" [See Isaiah 63:8.] He looks for fair-dealing, you see, at your hands. Whom may a father trust with his reputation, if not a child? Where can a prince expect honour, if not among his courtiers and favourites? Your state is such as the least mercy you have is more than all the world besides. Thou, Christian, and thy few brethren, divide heaven and earth among you. What hath God that he withholds from you? Sun, moon, and stars are set up to give you light, sea and land have their treasures and store for your use. Others do but ravish them; you are the rightful heirs to them. They groan that any other should be served by them. The angels, bad and good, minister unto you; the evil, against their will, are forced, like scullions, when they tempt you, to scour and brighten your graces, and make way for your greater comforts. ...The good angels are servants to your heavenly Father, and disdain not to

carry you in their arms. Your God withholds not himself from you. He is your portion, father, husband, friend, and what not. ...God is his own happiness, and admits you to enjoy himself. O what honour is this, for the subject to drink in his prince's cup! "*Thou shalt make them drink of the river of thy pleasures.*" [Psalm 36:8 KJV.] And all this, not as the purchase of your sweat, much less blood; the feast is paid for by another hand, and you are welcome: only he expects your thanks to the founder of it.... No sin-offering is imposed upon you under the gospel; thank-offerings are all he looks for.[14]

Stephen Charnock, in discoursing on spiritual worship, said,

The praise of God is the choicest sacrifice and worship under a dispensation of redeeming grace; this is the prime and eternal part of worship under the gospel. The Psalmist, speaking of the gospel times, spurs on to this kind of worship: "Sing to the Lord a new song; let the children of Zion be joyful in their king; let the saints be joyful in glory, and sing aloud on their beds; let the high praises of God be in their mouths" [Psalm 149:1–2, 5–6]; he begins and ends...with "Praise ye the Lord." That cannot be a spiritual and evangelical worship, that hath nothing of the praise of God in the heart. The consideration of God's adorable perfections, discovered in the gospel, will make us come to him with more seriousness; beg blessings of him with more confidence; fly to him with a winged faith and love, and more spiritually glorify him in our attendance upon him.[15]

There is a great deal more said in the Bible about praise than prayer, yet how few praise meetings there are! David, in his psalms, always mixed praise with prayer. Solomon prevailed much with God in prayer

---

14. William Gurnall, *The Christian in Complete Armour* (London: Blackie and Son, 1865), 67.
15. Stephen Charnock, *Discourses upon the Existence and Attributes of God* (New York: Robert Carter & Brothers, 1874), 233–234.

at the dedication of the temple, but it was the voice of praise that brought down the glory that filled the house, for we read,

> *And it came to pass, when the priests were come out of the holy place: (for all the priests that were present were sanctified, and did not then wait by course: also the Levites which were the singers, all them of Asaph and Heman, of Jeduthun, with their sons and their brethren, being arrayed in white linen, having cymbals and psalteries and harps, stood at the east end of the altar, and with them a hundred and twenty priests sounding with trumpets:) it came even to pass, as the trumpeters and singers were as one, to make one sound to be heard in praising and thanking the LORD; and when they lifted up their voice with the trumpets and cymbals and instruments of music, and praised the LORD, saying, For He is good; for His mercy endures for ever: that then the house was filled with a cloud, even the house of the LORD; so that the priests could not stand to minister by reason of the cloud: for the glory of the LORD had filled the house of God.*   (2 Chronicles 5:11–14)

We read, too, of Jehoshaphat, that he gained the victory over the hosts of Ammon and Moab through praise, which was excited by faith and thankfulness to God:

> *And they rose early in the morning, and went forth into the wilderness of Tekoa: and as they went forth, Jehoshaphat stood and said, Hear me, O Judah, and you inhabitants of Jerusalem; Believe in the LORD your God, so shall you be established; believe His prophets, so shall you prosper. And when he had consulted with the people, he appointed singers to the LORD, and that should praise the beauty of holiness, as they went out before the army, and to say, Praise the LORD; for His mercy endures for ever. And when they began to sing and to praise, the LORD set ambushments against the children of Ammon, Moab, and mount Seir, which were come against Judah; and they were smitten.*   (2 Chronicles 20:20–22)

It is said that in a time of great despondency among the first settlers in New England, it was proposed in one of their public assemblies to proclaim a fast. An old farmer arose. He spoke of their provoking heaven with their complaints. He reviewed their measures, showed that they had much to be thankful for, and moved that instead of appointing a day of fasting, they should appoint a day of thanksgiving. This was done, and the custom has been continued ever since.

However great our difficulties, however deep our sorrows, there is room for thankfulness. Thomas Adams said,

> Lay up in the ark of thy memory not only the pot of manna, the bread of life; but even Aaron's rod, the very scourge of correction, wherewith you have been bettered. Blessed be the Lord, not only giving, but taking away, said Job. (See Job 1:21.) God, who sees there is no walking upon roses to heaven, puts His children into the way of discipline and by the fire of correction eats out the rust of corruption. God sends trouble; then He bids us call upon Him; He promises our deliverance; and lastly, the all [the only thing] He requires of us is to glorify Him. *"Call upon me in the day of trouble; I will deliver you, and you shall glorify me"* [Psalm 50:15].

Like the nightingale, we can sing in the night, and we can say with John Newton,

> Since all that I meet shall work for my good,
> The bitter is sweet, the medicine food;
> Though painful at present, will cease before long,
> And then, O! how glorious, the conqueror's song.

Among all the apostles, none suffered as much as Paul, but none of them do we find giving thanks as often as he. Take his letter to the Philippians for an example. Remember what he suffered at Philippi, how they beat him with many blows and cast him into prison. Yet every chapter in this epistle speaks of rejoicing and giving thanks. There is this well-known passage:

> *Be careful for nothing; but in every thing by prayer and supplication with thanksgiving let your requests be made known to God.*
>
> (Philippians 4:6)

As someone once said, there are, in this verse, three precious ideas: "Anxious for nothing; prayerful for everything; and thankful for anything." We always get more by being thankful for what God has done for us.

Paul also said, "*We give thanks to God and the Father of our Lord Jesus Christ, praying always for you*" (Colossians 1:3). He was constantly giving thanks. Look at any one of his epistles, and you will find them full of praise to God.

Even if we had nothing else to be thankful for, we would always have ample cause for giving thanks in that Jesus Christ loved us and gave Himself for us. (See Galatians 2:20.)

A farmer was once found kneeling at a soldier's grave near Nashville. Someone came to him and said, "Why do you pay so much attention to this grave? Was your son buried here?"

"No," he said. "During the war my family was all sick; I knew not how I could leave them. I was drafted. One of my neighbors came over and said, 'I will go for you; I have no family.' He went off. He was wounded at Chickamauga. He was carried to the hospital and there died. And, sir, I have come many miles so that I might write over his grave these words: 'He died for me.'"

Believers can always say of our blessed Savior the same thing, and we can greatly rejoice in this fact. "*By Him therefore let us offer the sacrifice of praise to God continually, that is, the fruit of our lips giving thanks to His name*" (Hebrews 13:15).

22

THE PRAYER OF FAITH

Charles Finney

Therefore I say to you, What things soever you desire, when you pray, believe that you receive them, and you shall have them.
                                                                (Mark 11:24)

There are general promises and principles laid down in the Bible that Christians would have the opportunity to use, if they would only think. Whenever you are in circumstances to which the promises or principles apply, you are to use them.

A parent can find this promise:

The mercy of the LORD is from everlasting to everlasting upon them that fear Him, and His righteousness to children's children; to such as keep His covenant, and to those that remember His commandments to do them.   (Psalm 103:17–18)

This is a promise made to those who possess a certain character. If any parent knows he has this character, he can justifiably apply this promise to himself and his family. If you have this character, you are bound to make use of this promise in prayer and to believe it even for your children's children.

WHEN TO PRAY IN FAITH

Where there is any prophetic declaration that something prayed for is agreeable to the will of God, when it is plain from prophecy that the event is certainly to come, you are bound to believe it and to make it the basis of your special faith in prayer. If the time is not specified in the Bible and there is no indication of time from other sources, you are not bound to believe that it will take place in the near future. But if the time is specified, if it can be learned from studying the prophecies, and if it appears to have arrived, then Christians must understand and apply it by offering the prayer of faith.

For instance, take the case of Daniel and the return of the Jews from captivity. What did Daniel say? *"I Daniel understood by books the number of the years, whereof the word of the LORD came to Jeremiah the prophet, that He would accomplish seventy years in the desolations of Jerusalem"* (Daniel 9:2). He studied his Bible and understood that the length of the captivity was to be seventy years.

What did he do then? Did he sit down on the promise and say, "God has pledged Himself to put an end to the captivity in seventy years; the time has expired, and there is no need to do anything"? Oh, no. He said, *"And I set my face to the Lord God, to seek by prayer and supplications, with fasting, and sackcloth, and ashes"* (verse 3). He set himself at once to pray that the end of the captivity would come to pass. He prayed in faith.

But what was he to believe? He believed what he learned from the prophecy. There are many prophecies yet unfulfilled in the Bible that Christians should try to understand as far as they are capable. They are then to make the prophecies the basis of believing prayer. Do not think, as some seem to, that because something is foretold in prophecy, that it is not necessary to pray for it, or that it will come whether Christians pray for it or not. God says, in regard to as yet unfulfilled events that are revealed in prophecy: *"I will yet for this be inquired of by the house of Israel, to do it for them"* (Ezekiel 36:37).

TRUSTING THE SPIRIT'S LEADING

When the Spirit of God is upon You and excites strong desires for any blessing, you are bound to pray for it in faith. You are bound to infer, from the fact that you find yourself drawn to desire such a thing while experiencing the joy and holiness the Spirit of God produces, that these desires are the work of the Spirit. People are not likely to desire with the right kind of desires unless they are inspired by the Spirit of God. The apostle referred to these desires, excited by the Spirit, in his epistle to the Romans, where he said, *"Likewise the Spirit also helps our infirmities: for we know not what we should pray for as we ought: but the Spirit Itself makes intercession for us with groanings which cannot be uttered"* (Romans 8:26).

It is clear that the prayer of faith will obtain the blessing because our faith rests on evidence that it is the will of God to grant the thing. The Scripture is not evidence that something else will be granted, but that this particular thing will be.

THE FRUIT OF FAITHFUL PRAYER

People often receive more than they pray for. Solomon prayed for wisdom, and God granted him riches and honor in addition. Similarly, a wife may pray for the conversion of her husband, and if she offers the prayer in faith, God may not only grant that blessing, but also convert her child and her whole family. (See Acts 16:31.) Blessings sometimes seem to "hang together," so that if a Christian gains one, he gains them all.

I could name many individuals who decided to examine the Bible on this subject, and who, before they were through with it, were filled with the spirit of prayer. They found that God meant just what a plain, commonsense man would understand Him to mean. I advise you to try it. You have Bibles. Look them over; and whenever you find a promise you can use, plant it in your mind before you go on. You will not get through the Book without finding out that God's promises mean just what they say.

GIVING UP TOO SOON

You must persevere. You are not to pray for a thing once, then cease, and call that the prayer of faith. Look at Daniel. He prayed for twentyone days and did not stop until he obtained the blessing. He set his heart and face toward the Lord to seek His answer by prayer and supplication. He held on for three weeks, and then the answer came. And why did it not come before? God sent an archangel with the message, but the devil hindered him. (See Daniel 10:10–14.) See what Christ said in the parable of the unjust judge and the parable of the loaves. What did He teach us by them? He taught that God will grant answers to prayer when prayer is persistent. *"Shall not God avenge His own elect, which cry day and night to Him...?"* (Luke 18:7).

A PREVAILING PRINCE OF PRAYER

Once a good man said to me, "Oh, I am dying of a lack of strength to pray! My body is crushed; the world is on me; how can I continue praying?" I have known that man to go to bed absolutely sick because of weakness and faintness under the pressure. And I have known him to pray as if he would do violence to heaven, and then I have seen the blessing come as plainly in answer to his prayer as if it were revealed. No person would doubt it any more than if God spoke from heaven.

This is how he died. He prayed more and more. He used to take the map of the world, look over the different countries, and pray for them until he collapsed in his room. Blessed man! He was the reproach of the ungodly and of carnal Christians. But he was the favorite of heaven and a prevailing prince in prayer.

"But," you ask, "for whom are we to pray this prayer? We want to know which cases, which people, which places, and at what times we are to pray the prayer of faith." I answer, as I have already answered, "When you have evidence—from providences, promises, prophecies, or the leadings of the Spirit—that God will do the things for which you pray."

GOD'S PROMISE TO PARENTS

You may also ask, "Did you not say there is a promise that Christian parents may apply to their children? Why is it, then, that so many faithful parents have had impenitent children who died in their sins?" This is often the case, but it proves a point, especially in view of Romans 3:4: *"Let God be true, but every man a liar."* Will we believe that God has not kept His promise or that these parents did not do their duty? Perhaps they did not believe the promise or did not believe there was any such thing as the prayer of faith. Wherever you find a Christian who does not believe in any such prayer, you find in general that he has children yet in their sins.

"But," you ask, "will these views lead to fanaticism? Will people think they are offering the prayer of faith when they are not?" This is an argument against all spiritual religion whatsoever. Some people think they have it when they do not, and they are fanatics. But there are those who know what the prayer of faith is, just as there are those who know what spiritual experience is, though such prayer may be a stumbling block to coldhearted believers who do not know it. Even ministers often leave themselves open to the rebuke that Christ gave to Nicodemus: *"Are you a master of Israel, and know not these things?"* (John 3:10).

UNDERSTANDING THE PRAYER OF FAITH

People who have not known by experience what the prayer of faith is have good reason to doubt their own piety. This statement is by no means unkind. Let them examine themselves. It is likely that they understand prayer as little as Nicodemus understood the new birth. (See John 3:1–9.) They have not walked with God. You cannot accurately describe the walk to them any more than you can describe a beautiful painting to a blind man.

There is reason to believe that millions are in hell because Christians have not offered the prayer of faith on their behalf. In some instances, when believers had promises under their noses, they did not have enough faith to use them. The signs of the times and the indications of providence were favorable, perhaps, and the Spirit of God prompted desires for the salvation of souls. There was evidence enough that God was ready to grant a blessing, and if Christians had only prayed in faith, God would have granted it. But He turned it away because they would not discern the signs of the times.

WHEN TO EXPECT AN ANSWER

I knew a father who was a good man, but who had misconceptions about the prayer of faith. His whole family of children were grown up, without one of them being converted. One day his son grew ill and seemed ready to die. The father prayed, but the son grew worse and was sinking into the grave without hope. The father prayed until his anguish was unutterable. Finally, when there seemed no prospect of his son surviving, he poured out his soul to God as if he would not be denied.

Later, he got an assurance that his son would not only live, but also be converted. In addition, God assured him that not only this one, but also his whole family would be converted to God. He came into the house and told his family that his son would not die. They were astonished at him. "I tell you," he said, "he will not die. And no child of mine will ever die in his sins." That man's children were all converted years ago.

What do you think of that? Was that fanaticism? If you believe it was, it is because you know nothing about the prayer of faith. Do you pray like this man prayed? Do you live in such a manner that you can offer such prayers for your children? I know that children of Christians may sometimes be converted in answer to the prayers of someone else. But do you dare leave your children to the prayers of others, when God calls you to sustain this important duty to your children?

BELIEVING THE GOOD BOOK

In conclusion, think about the efforts people are making to dispose of the Bible completely. The unsaved are in favor of doing away with the warnings of the Bible, and the church wants to do away with its promises. What does that leave? Without these, the Bible would be an empty book. I ask in love, what is our Bible good for if we do not take hold of its precious promises and use them as the ground of our faith when we pray for the blessing of God? You would do better to send your Bibles to the nonChristians, where they will do some good, if you are not going to believe and use them.

BIBLIOGRAPHY

Books Excerpted for This Volume

Bounds, E. M., *Answered Prayer*. New Kensington, PA: Whitaker House, 2002.

Bounds, E. M., *Power Through Prayer*. New Kensington, PA: Whitaker House, 1983.

Bounds, E. M., *The Essentials of Prayer*. New Kensington, PA: Whitaker House, 1994.

Bounds, E. M., *The Necessity of Prayer*. New Kensington, PA: Whitaker House, 2013.

Finney, Charles, *How to Experience Revival*. New Kensington, PA: Whitaker House, 2017.

Moody, D. L., *The Joy of Answered Prayer*. New Kensington, PA: Whitaker House, 2002.

Müller, George, *Release the Power of Prayer*. New Kensington, PA: Whitaker House, 2005.

Murray, Andrew, *Prayer Life*. New Kensington, PA: Whitaker House, 2018.

Spurgeon, C. H., *Power in Prayer*. New Kensington, PA: Whitaker House, 2017.

Spurgeon, C. H., *Prayer*. New Kensington, PA: Whitaker House, 2001.

Spurgeon, C. H., *Praying Successfully*. New Kensington, PA: Whitaker House, 1997.

Torrey, R. A., *How to Pray*. New Kensington, PA: Whitaker House, 1983.

Torrey, R. A., *The Power of Prayer*. New Kensington, PA: Whitaker House, 2000.

ABOUT THE AUTHORS

Edward McKendree Bounds (1835–1913) was born in a small northeastern Missouri town. An avid reader of the Scriptures and an ardent admirer of John Wesley's sermons, Bounds practiced law until the age of twenty-four, when he suddenly felt called to preach the gospel. His first pastorate was in the nearby town of Monticello, Missouri. Yet, in 1861, while he was pastor of a Methodist Episcopal church in Brunswick, the Civil War began, and Bounds was arrested by Union troops and charged for sympathizing with the Confederacy. After the war, Bounds pastored churches in Nashville, Tennessee; Selma, Alabama; and St. Louis, Missouri. While in St. Louis, Bounds accepted a position as associate editor for the regional Methodist journal, the *St. Louis Advocate*. Then, after only nineteen months, he moved to Nashville to become the editor of the *Christian Advocate*, the weekly paper for the entire Methodist Episcopal denomination in the South. The final seventeen years of his life were spent with his family in Washington, Georgia. Most of the time he spent reading, writing, and praying, but he often took an active part in revival ministry. Bounds was also in the habit of rising at four o'clock each morning in order to pray to God, for the great cares of the world were always upon his heart. He died on August 24, 1913, still relatively unknown to most of the Christian sphere. He is known for writing eleven books, nine of which focused on the subject of prayer, including E. M. *Bounds on Prayer, Essentials of Prayer, Necessity of Prayer, Power Through Prayer*, and many others.

Charles G. Finney (1792–1875) was a man with a message that burned through the religious deadwood and secular darkness of his time. He had the ability to shock both saint and sinner alike. Because he was radical in both his methods and his message, Finney was criticized for almost everything except being boring. Born in Connecticut in 1792, Finney was nearly thirty years of age when he turned from his skepticism regarding Christianity and wholeheartedly embraced the Bible as the true Word of God. He gave up his law profession in order to spread the gospel, and he soon became the most noteworthy revivalist of the nineteenth century, one of the leaders of the Second Great Awakening. It is estimated that over 250,000 souls were converted as a result of his preaching. While Finney carried his revivals to several middle and eastern states, the bulk of his meetings were in New York towns. Finney established the theology department at Oberlin Collegiate Institute (known today as Oberlin College). He served there as a professor of theology, as well as pastor of Oberlin's First Congregational Church, until a few years before his death. During these years, he continued to carry on his evangelism, even visiting Great Britain twice in 1849–50 and 1859–60.

Dwight Lyman Moody (1837–1899) started life as a successful shoe salesman but became one of the most respected evangelists of the nineteenth century. In his early years, he was known for his highly effective Sunday school ministry and his evangelistic work among soldiers during the Civil War. After Moody's church was destroyed in the Great Chicago Fire, he received a powerful infilling of the Holy Spirit. Newly empowered, he held dynamic meetings in America and Great Britain and founded Moody Bible Institute. When he died, Moody left a rich legacy: three Christian schools, a Christian publishing business, and a million souls won for Christ.

George Müller (1805–1898) was born in Kroppenstaedt, Prussia, on September 27, 1805. He was the son of a tax collector, and, before he became a Christian, he had the reputation of being a liar and a thief. After accepting Christ as his personal Savior, he was used in remarkable ways to provide for more than ten thousand orphans during his lifetime. He never went into debt or asked anyone to supply his needs. He trusted in God to provide for him and for the orphans, and God never failed to do so. In 1875, he began preaching tours that took him over 200,000 miles to forty-two countries to preach to three million people. God transformed a little boy who stole from his earthly father into a man who could be trusted with the resources of his heavenly Father. The ministry of George Müller continues today through the establishment of the George Müller Foundation.

Andrew Murray (1828–1917) was an amazingly prolific Christian writer. He lived and ministered as both a pastor and author in the towns and villages of South Africa. He wrote to give daily practical help to many of the people in his congregation who lived out in the farming communities and could come into town for church services only on rare occasions. Some of Murray's earliest works were written to provide nurture and guidance to Christians, whether young or old in the faith; they were actually an extension of his pastoral work. Once books such as *Abide in Christ*, *Divine Healing*, and *With Christ in the School of Prayer* were written, Murray became widely known, and new books from his pen were awaited with great eagerness throughout the world.

Charles Haddon Spurgeon (1834–1892), the "Prince of Preachers," preached his first sermon at age sixteen. During his lifetime he preached to an estimated ten million people. He founded and supported charitable outreaches, including educational institutions. He also founded a pastors' college and the famous Stockwell Orphanage. Spurgeon published over two thousand of his sermons, as well as numerous books, which compose the largest collection of work by a single author. Highlighted with splashes of spontaneous, delightful humor, his teachings still provide direction to all who are seeking true joy and genuine intimacy with God.

Reuben Archer Torrey (1856–1928) was one of the greatest evangelists of the twentieth century. Several years after his graduation from Yale Divinity School, he was selected by D. L. Moody to become the first dean of the Moody Bible Institute of Chicago. Under his direction, Moody Institute became a pattern for Bible institutes around the world. From 1903 to 1905, Dr. Torrey traveled the world in revival campaigns, winning thousands of souls to Jesus Christ. He continued worldwide crusades for the next fifteen years while he served as the dean of the Bible Institute of Los Angeles and pastored that city's Church of the Open Door. Dr. Torrey longed for more Christian workers to take an active part in bringing the message of salvation through Christ to a lost and dying world. His straightforward style of evangelism has shown thousands of Christian workers how to become effective soulwinners.

Welcome to Our House!

We Have a Special Gift for You ...

It is our privilege and pleasure to share in your love of Christian classics by publishing books that enrich your life and encourage your faith.

To show our appreciation, we invite you to sign up to receive a specially selected **Reader Appreciation Gift**, with our compliments. Just go to the Web address at the bottom of this page.

God bless you as you seek a deeper walk with Him!

WE HAVE A GIFT FOR YOU

whpub.me/classicthx

WHITAKER
HOUSE